GUILTY LAND

PATRICK VAN RENSBURG

GUILTY LAND

The History of Apartheid

FREDERICK A. PRAEGER, *Publisher*
New York

BOOKS THAT MATTER

PUBLISHED IN THE UNITED STATES OF AMERICA IN 1962
BY FREDERICK A. PRAEGER, INC., PUBLISHER
64 UNIVERSITY PLACE, NEW YORK 3, N.Y.

LIBRARY OF CONGRESS CATALOG CARD NUMBER: 62 : 9588

PRINTED IN GREAT BRITAIN

CONTENTS

ACKNOWLEDGMENTS

I am greatly indebted to Mrs Pat Williams for the help and advice she gave me in the writing of this book. I am also grateful to H. R. for his advice and for the many valuable changes he suggested, and to Miss Beryl Longley and Mrs Margaret Anderson for typing the manuscript in its various stages.

The Oxford University Press has given me permission to quote from *Civil Liberty in South Africa,* by Edgar Brookes and J. B. Macauley. Mr Ronald Segal has allowed quotations from the quarterly *Africa South.* At various places in the book I have referred to three other books, without acknowledging the publishers. They are *Africa's Challenge to America,* by Chester Bowles — the University of California Press; *Shooting at Sharpeville,* by the Rt Rev. Ambrose Reeves — Victor Gollancz; and *South Africa and World Opinion,* by Peter Calvocoressi — published by the Oxford University Press under the auspices of the Institute of Race Relations.

P. v. R.

PART ONE

A TRAITOR TO HATRED

CHAPTER I

A TRAITOR TO HATRED

O
N the night of March 30th, 1960, I fled from South Africa to Swaziland to seek political asylum from the Government of South Africa. Until May 31st, 1957, I had served that same Government loyally and to the best of my ability as Vice-Consul in Leopoldville. In less than three years, I had graduated from being a servant of the Government to being one of its extremest opponents. I was regarded by nearly all Afrikaners as a traitor and treated as such.

This book is not about myself. But I changed so radically in so short a time that there may be some value in examining the reasons. Perhaps, in describing those events in my life which did most to make me change, I can throw a little more light on the tragedy of misunderstanding that has unfolded in South Africa, where a frightened people have become committed to a course of action, and are unable to see how the present attempt to safeguard their future is the very factor most likely to destroy it.

I was born in Durban in December 1931, and shortly after my birth my parents separated. My mother had to go out to work and her job took her away from Durban, so she left me with my grandmother. It was my grandmother who brought me up, but not as an Afrikaner, although she herself was one. I was seventeen when I first began to think of myself as an Afrikaner and to wonder why I had been denied an Afrikaans upbringing.

My grandmother was crippled by rheumatism and unable to bend her left leg. She made a comfortable living for both of us by taking in boarders and by dressmaking. And she was helped

financially by my father, whom I very rarely saw, and her un-
married son.

As a girl during the Boer War, she had been in a British concentration camp. Then she settled in Natal and married my
French-speaking grandfather from Mauritius. They too were
separated, but the marriage had left its mark in that my grandmother had taken her husband's religion, Roman Catholicism,
and shed most of her links with Afrikanerdom. She was an ardent
supporter of Smuts, and an implacable foe of Afrikaner political
nationalism, but she hardly ever spoke to me directly about our
country's politics or history, nor even about her own upbringing.

She was a big woman, with a domineering personality and a
very quick temper. She did not hesitate to beat me on the many
occasions when she felt it necessary. She had had little formal
education and was essentially a very simple person, inclined to
sentimentality, and on the whole kind and generous.

I vividly recall an incident shortly before her death, when she
and I had stayed on at the dinner-table one evening, chatting to
two of her boarders. They were a newly married couple, both
Afrikaner nationalists. (The husband was a railway worker. The
young wife had taught me more about Afrikanerdom than I had
ever learned from my grandmother.) That evening the conversation was about the strife between the two White language groups.
The Boer War inevitably featured in the discussion, and with it
the British maltreatment of Afrikaner women and children in the
concentration camps. When it cropped up, my grandmother became livid with rage. She banged the table with the walking-stick
she always carried.

'Have *you* ever been in one of those concentration camps?' she
screamed. They had no answer. They were both born at least
twenty-five years after the whole thing was over. 'Well, I have,' she
went on, shaking with .emotion. She spiritedly denied the charges
of cruelty that they had made. But what rankled with her most
was that she, who had been an inmate of a concentration camp,
could have forgotten and forgiven, while these people, born a full

generation later, should summon up the ghosts of the past to sustain their present hatreds. She was so angry that she would not allow them to continue the argument. I knew better than to try to ask them further questions, and out of sheer filial devotion I took her side. I was ten or eleven at the time, and this conversation lingered in my mind like a question mark. It was my first introduction to the politics of the White language groups of South Africa.

Outside our home, my setting was that of White Natal. People there have strong anti-Indian and anti-Afrikaner prejudices. One 'liked the native', who, one believed, in turn 'liked' us. He was, we thought, 'perfectly happy', sitting and laughing in the sun. He was lazy and unambitious, but what right had we to impose 'our way of life' on him? We genuinely believed that 'the natives' were happy as domestics and factory workers — simply because they really did seem to be for ever smiling. As far as one can generalize, the Africans are by nature a gracious, smiling people, and this certainly created an impression of contentment. Today, the smiles are less frequent and the graciousness is tempered by bitterness. But today is a far cry from those misleading days.

One of the most frequently heard remarks from White South Africans, now as then, is, 'I like the "old" type of native. He is courteous, polite, and knows his place. But these young, half-educated city slickers are a bad lot. They are the ones who cause all the trouble.'

At school we spoke of the African as 'Jim Fish', the 'Munt', or the 'Coon'; the Indians were the 'Coolies' or the 'Churrahs'; the Afrikaners the 'Boets', 'Jaaps' or 'Backvelders'; the Coloureds (or Eurafricans) the 'Koetchies'; and the Jews the 'Yids'. In our own house, Johannesburg was often called 'Jewsburg'. I remember at high school how one Jewish boy was unmercifully and continuously ragged, and taunted with being a Jew. He was an odd child who would probably have been ragged in any case, but the racial slander was significant. I never questioned any of these attitudes. This was what the world was like.

In their younger days my grandparents had lived in Avoca, a small town on the north coast of Natal. There was a substantial Indian community there. Of all the underprivileged, subjugated racial groups in Natal, it is the Indians who have been in the strongest and most direct economic competition with the Whites. A small minority, less than fifteen per cent, control powerful economic interests; a growing number are improving as technicians, artisans and clerks; but the vast majority of them are poor and engaged in market-gardening and door-to-door vegetable selling.

At Avoca a handful of Indians owned sugar-cane farms, and many of the others worked on such farms, owned either by Indians or Europeans. A fair number of Mauritians live in this area because of the sugar farming, since the principal product of Mauritius is sugar, and many of them are of mixed racial origin. My grandfather was then a railway ticket inspector, and it was a point of pride in our family that he was racially 'pure'. It was in this environment that my grandmother's traditional racial consciousness found its expression. She knew exactly who was 'pure White' and who was not. A Mauritian family were our near neighbours, but she forbade me to play with the children: they were 'not quite White'. Some of these people were infinitely richer than we were, but we were able to keep our heads high. We were White.

My grandfather's relatives — also poor White Mauritians — maintained their friendship with my grandmother, despite her separation from her husband. They all felt rather as she did about the Mauritians. There is a large Indian population in Mauritius, and my relatives had brought with them a traditional attitude towards these people; that is to say, they despised the richer Indians more than the poorer ones. Whenever we saw Indians living in decent houses, there was always the same comment: 'They are so filthy. Look how dirty they make their houses!' My grandmother was far more generous towards the Indian vegetable hawker who came to the door. It was no threat to our pride to talk to him. He did not expect to be asked into the sitting-room. In no sense would we ever think of these people as our equals. I vividly recall that when I was nine or ten, a relative by marriage, an Englishwoman and an exquisite confectioner, had baked a cake and beautifully decorated it with pink icing that looked just like fine lace. The family was raffling it for some cause or other and the winning ticket was in the name of the hawker. He had bought it for sixpence while selling his vegetables, but everyone in the family agreed, when the raffle was drawn, that the hawker would not appreciate the cake and that it would be a waste to let him have it. So there was another draw and a white person came up as winner.

We always bought our vegetables from these Indian hawkers, who came to our door, and my grandmother drove a hard bargain with them. Still, she had a relaxed and fairly understanding relationship with one Indian woman who came frequently. And I was allowed long conversations with the butcher's delivery boy, also an Indian, in which she sometimes joined. They were mostly about horse-racing. The legend was that every Indian had inside information about the horses.

Thus we assembled our stereotypes. Like most South Africans, we knew nothing about the lives of these people; nothing except a few superficial facts — but from these we built up images. It was the same with the African servants. We were always conscious of the fact that they were right at the bottom of the social scale, so conscious of it that we never stopped to think. They were simply there. We had a long succession of domestic servants: they were either lazy, or they stole, or they brewed 'kaffir beer' illicitly and the stench attracted policemen on patrol; or they broke crockery (deliberately), or they had boy-friends living on the premises. We were convinced of their ingrained, inherent immorality and inefficiency, although we were kind to them, in our fashion. We gave them extra food, or money, or occasional old clothes. We were also convinced they were ungrateful, because, despite our kindness, they would steal more food than we gave them, or pinch my uncle's tobacco or liquor.

GUILTY LAND

Throughout my schooldays I bore my grandmother's married name, Lagesse. It happened quite by accident. I regarded her as my mother and addressed her as such, and anyone who had anything to do with us assumed that she was. I rarely saw my real mother, whom I addressed by her Christian name. By now, my childhood name had become anglicized and was pronounced 'Lar-jess'. Consequently I escaped being thought of as an Afrikaner, and indeed hardly considered myself one. I was therefore never abused as an Afrikaner; on the contrary, I joined in abusing them until well after the concentration camp conversation had raised questions in my mind.

Natal has always been predominantly English-speaking, but between the two world wars the Hertzog Afrikaner Government imported into Natal a large number of Afrikaans-speaking people, in order to increase contact between the two groups. Unfortunately they brought in civil servants and railway workers, poorer people who hardly represented a true cross-section of their group, and were as a whole unlikely to make a particularly good impression on English-speaking Natal. The only Afrikaners I knew, apart from my anglicized grandmother and innumerable others equally anglicized, were the two young nationalists who boarded with us. However, neither of these people conditioned my view of the Afrikaner; it was conditioned rather by the boys who attended the local Afrikaans-language school, whom we saw in the bus or in the street. We fought a sort of running battle with them; one of the differences between us was that they spoke the language we were forced to learn at school. Invariably they had close-cropped haircuts and pug noses. I was influenced too by the men I saw at the Railway Institute when my uncle went in for a drink on a Sunday, leaving me waiting an hour or so in his car. They also had close-cropped heads of hair, wore their national uniform of flannels and sports coats that hung half-way up their backs, and looked somehow unlike any other Whites.

I saw my birth certificate for the first time soon after I left school, when I needed it in applying for a job. My grandmother

16

had been dead for nearly four years, and the powerful emotional influence of a mother on her child had almost disappeared. The Afrikaner Nationalist Government had been in power for the best part of a year, and the shock of their unexpected and dramatic election (which I felt chiefly because my elders did) had — so far as I was concerned — given way to an inquisitive interest. I was only now properly discovering the Nationalist Party and its creed. In this state of mind, I learned that I was van Rensburg, and I felt that something had been withheld from me and denied me.

I had been uncertain as to what to do for a living. I should have liked to attend university, but could not afford it. I had contemplated becoming a teacher and accepting a loan from the education department of the provincial government to cover my training. I also had a long-standing interest in journalism. In the end, because I had a vague feeling of wanting to do something of public service, I was deluded into thinking that I could best fulfil this need by joining the civil service. My headmaster strongly advised me against becoming a teacher. 'You'll be wasting your talents,' he said. This flattered me enormously, and might well have misled me. I had recently gained prizes in two public essay competitions, and had attracted his attention and interest by this and one or two unorthodox extra-curricular activities. In fact, I drifted into the public service. I had to see a magistrate in Durban about joining, and he told me that I should revert to the name of my birth. It was largely from a strange and uncertain sense of pride that, on his advice, I did so. Legally, I could have kept the name I was known by.

There were more Afrikaners than English-speakers in the office of the Master of the Supreme Court, to which I was appointed. Among them I made two valuable friends. The Assistant Master, Mr J. J. A. Nel, was a tall, brilliant, middle-aged man, with a slight stoop and a balding head. He immediately took a fatherly interest in me, was always available to me, even though I was a very junior official, and spent hours in teaching me the finer details of my work. He encouraged me to wrestle with all the legal problems that cropped up and to argue them to a conclusion. Mr Nel also took a sympathetic interest in my personal problems, drew me out on them, and gave me advice. He was a quiet-spoken man, intense and serious, with a deep passion for good music. His one weakness — an endearing one — was for Tarzan films. When I began studying for an extra-mural degree, he kept me going with encouragement and interest. He drew me very gently towards a deeper understanding of and a greater sympathy for Afrikanerdom, and I suspect that he will be immensely sad about the course I have chosen in life.

My other friend was Daan van Tonder, a much younger and very different sort of man. He did not have anything like the insight, devotion and intensity of Mr Nel, but he was a passionate nationalist. We argued constantly about politics, and his grudges were real. As a good Afrikaner nationalist, he had refused to fight in the war against Hitler and had been penalized. He argued well, if superficially, and spoke with no personal bitterness, despite his grudges. We shared an office, and he was always at hand to explain the unfolding Afrikaner Nationalist Government's policy. There was nothing gentle about his attempt to win me over to Afrikanerdom, and there was a faint hint of emotional blackmail in his talk. When speaking to me of others like me, he hinted at the 'renegade'.

There was yet a third more personal and less permanent influence during that first working year of mine. In our office was a young Afrikaner girl from the Orange Free State, the heartland of Afrikaner nationalism, and she added a strong emotional stimulus to my growing interest in Afrikanerdom.

These three people began to shatter all my misconceptions and preconceptions about Afrikaners.

During that first year I was taking a correspondence course in Afrikaans-Nederlands towards my degree. I was learning in greater detail about the growth of Afrikaans and of Afrikaans literature, and more especially about its beautiful poetry. What I learned was made more meaningful by my contact with people like Mr Nel — and the girl, Johanna Roos.

When Daan van Tonder took me to the Orange Free State to his brother's wedding, it was an exciting experience. I had never before left Natal, and now my first escape was right into the bosom of Afrikaner nationalism. I remember, as if it happened yesterday, the strange feeling I had at the reception as I noticed how very much these people looked like the people I had mixed with in Natal. Afrikaners were *not* all pug-faced people with short hair-cuts! There were good-looking men and beautiful girls, just as there were among the people I associated with at home. It struck me like a blow in the face, and when I talked with them after-wards and danced in the evening with the girls, the transformation was complete. We spent the rest of the week-end with Daan's mother, and she reminded me of my grandmother. She had the same grey hair, the same kind of voice. I felt at home.

The second time I left Natal, not long afterwards, it was again to go to the Orange Free State with a Rugby football team touring three towns. Most of our own team were Afrikaners, and we were accommodated with Afrikaner families. We played together and revelled together, dancing in the evenings to the *tiekie-draai,* a fast-moving tune, rarely pretty, but with its own fascination, and we joined our hosts at the *vleisbraai,* where meat was grilled out-doors over an open fire — an Afrikaner tradition.

I was also studying history during this first year, and was learn-ing more about Afrikaner history than I had ever known before. My grandmother had been silent about it. At school it had been learnt without personal interest and without emotional involve-ment. Now I had the interest and the sympathy, and I sensed the grievances of a people whose wrongs had by no means ended with the Boer War. The official recognition of their language was the first fruit of Union, and they had a rightful sense of deep pride in it.

When the Voortrekker Monument was unveiled on December 16th, 1949, I spent the whole day beside a radio listening to the speeches. This was a monument to the heroic exploits of the

Voortrekkers, who were the ancestors of the modern Afrikaners, and who opened up the interior of southern Africa. I was hypnotized and spellbound by the fascinating oratory of Dr Malan as he constructed his vast 'Quo Vadis' speech. Later in this book I have quoted a little from that speech as I have come to see it, without the fascination and hypnotism, and away from its tribal witchcraft. That day it moved me deeply; today it distresses me deeply.

My first year out of school — 1949 — was a most confusing one. I was in the throes of this vast and sudden change. I was even ready to forsake the Roman Catholic Church for the Dutch Reformed Church, but my religion still had the stranglehold of childhood memories, and in the first stresses and strains of adult life I went scurrying back to it. Like Gerard Manley Hopkins, I was 'fleeing with a fling of the heart to the heart of the host'. Afrikanerdom and Roman Catholicism are not close friends in South Africa, and I had to struggle to reconcile them in my own mind. I had not cut myself off from my Natal background either, and my closest friends outside my office were typically English-speaking young men with the very attitudes I had been shuffling off.

Of the courses that I was taking for my degree, the one that was making the most impact on me was English. I was fascinated by the methods of Practical Criticism, which were opening up for me new worlds of perception and understanding. It was an unbelievable discovery. When I read now, there seemed to be vast realms of meaning which I hadn't previously seen; when I read again what I had read before it was like coming upon something new and different. I was no longer reading about pain and hurt to others; I was feeling it myself. I could understand the suffering Dickens was writing about; I felt that Hardy might have been talking to me.

I think it was then that I really learned compassion. In an odd sort of way I was learning to live, not only inwardly but outwardly also, understanding other people through myself. For me it was a great discovery and a new and rich experience. I might suddenly feel a rush of compassion for a man with a hole in his shoe or a frayed collar or a torn coat — things I was used to in myself — and though I would quickly brush it aside as sentimental ('That man doesn't need my sympathy'), in that brief moment I had had a fleeting glimpse of the truth that we are *all* tossed about in the same way, hoisted to heights of happiness and then dropped into depths of despair. When I later read the line from Shakespeare: 'One touch of nature makes the whole world kin', it struck home immediately.

I have said little that is new for others in this. For me it was not only new and different; it was revolutionary. It helped me immensely in getting to know and understand people better, and that included individual Afrikaners and — through them — their way of life. The Afrikaans poems that were a prescribed part of my course had by now become something that I read out of sheer enjoyment.

The Afrikaners are a tiny people up against the world. Even in their own world they are hopelessly outnumbered. They are one-and-three-quarter million of the three million Whites in a total population of fourteen million. As a nation they were born in South Africa, and as a nation they grew up there; they belong nowhere else. They have developed their own way of life and it differs even from that of the English-speaking Whites. They have their own language and their own history. They jealously guard their way of life because they think it worth guarding; it means, for one thing, the religion they believe in. Their politics demand the maintenance of their identity. In the past they have felt the maintenance of that identity threatened by the British, and more recently by the African. In guarding themselves against the British in 1900, they gained the sympathy of the world; in guarding themselves against the African in 1950, they have lost it.

I realize in retrospect that if at that time I was becoming a part of Afrikanerdom, it was not yet completely part of me. I went to it out of sympathy, in reaction to the slander against it, and having entered into the spirit, I found that it captivated me. But was

I so completely assimilated that I was blind to its excesses? How would I react if it were guilty of the very things which had been done against it, and which had led me to champion it? These questions did not arise then, but they have arisen since as I search the past, seeking the causes of my sympathy for African aspirations.

That I should have turned to Afrikanerdom was, in view of my earlier background, an essentially liberal action. The discovery of my blood ties with it made the process of conversion easier, and once I had come under its spell, the blood tie alone was enough to bind me there. But it was not inconceivable that I might feel the same sense of sympathy for any other group that was badly maligned.

In South Africa the White view of racial groups is so conditioned by politico-economic factors that when compassion for the African is felt at all, it is a free-floating, fragmented emotion. Most Whites who are at all sensitive may feel a fleeting moment of fellow-feeling for an individual African, but it will have to lie close to fear — fear of numbers, of what Africans want. This was my own state of mind when I was seventeen.

On the other hand, I detested the Indians. In January 1949, when the anti-Indian pogroms began and Africans in Durban killed many Indians, burning and looting their shops and homes and attacking them in the streets, I sat down gleefully to write a letter to the Natal Indian Congress. In it I asked if this was not surely their warning to leave South Africa and return to India. I had taken the fact that African anger was vented against the Indians, leaving the Whites untouched, as a sign that they were resented by both the Africans and us, and that it was clear that *we* and the Africans got on very well together. The riots did not spread to Pietermaritzburg, where I was then living, but one Sunday afternoon when I was driving with friends through the city's main street, I had a glimpse of an African running towards an elderly Indian, balancing himself on one foot with his arms raised to shoulder level, and kicking out and upwards at the old man's face. There was frenzy and hatred in the African's face, and the old Indian was petrified. I was disgusted at the time, but only as I might have been disgusted by cruelty, say, to a dog.

During the first two years of study, I spent a considerable amount of time at the local municipal library. I started going there once or twice a week to borrow books relevant to my studies — and then I discovered the reading-room. It soon became my habit, as a break from study, to spend an hour or two there browsing through all kinds of newspapers. Among the publications were some periodicals written by and for Africans; they found their way there because this was one of the statutory libraries to which all publishers are obliged by law to send all publications.

I was quite overwhelmed when I started reading these African journals; so much of their contents was clear, logical and well written. I was accustomed to thinking of Africans as domestic servants, factory workers, dock workers, labourers and performers of menial tasks. My only contacts with them were a youth's contacts with the household staff. As the greater part of my contact with new thought was through reading, so this particular disillusionment came through reading also. I have tried in vain to reconstruct just one line of what might have been said in those publications, but I have retained only the vague, over-all impression they made on me. Here were people asking for recognition as human beings, and meriting it because they were behaving as human beings. And when, at about this time, I read some of Shylock's lines in *The Merchant of Venice,* a few of the pieces began to fall into place:

He hath disgraced me, and hindered me half a million, laughed at my losses, mocked at my gains, scorned my nation, thwarted my bargains, cooled my friends, heated mine enemies; and what's his reason? I am a Jew. Hath not a Jew eyes? hath not a Jew hands, organs, dimensions, senses, affections, passions? fed with the same food, hurt with the same weapons, subject to the same diseases, healed by the same means, warmed and cooled by the same winter and summer as a Christian is? If you prick us do we not bleed?

It was precisely because this was completely in line with my own experience, and more particularly the experience of reading those African publications, that it suddenly struck me that Africans were really no different from us; that for our own reasons we had created the differences. That did not mean that the differences suddenly fell away, but I had broken through an emotional barrier and had a glimpse of the truth.

I had only just learnt to understand, respect and sympathize with the Afrikaner, and now already I was beginning to see the African in a new light. I knew the Afrikaner attitude to the African. How on earth could they be reconciled? I discussed some of my problem with friends at the office, especially with Daan van Tonder. He had very warm feelings for the Africans he knew, who were predominantly farm workers, respectful to their masters and a part of the traditional pattern of rural society. If he spoke with rancour, it was about the 'new class' of emergent Africans, a product of the conflict of traditional and modern values in the South African cities.

Daan van Tonder genuinely believed in apartheid, and he was a convincing advocate. Certainly its ideal of total physical separation of the races offered a way out of my dilemma, and a manner of being loyal both to Afrikanerdom and to my growing sympathy for the African. Since there was a history of conflict between the Afrikaner and the African, I reasoned, was it any less ethical to keep them apart than it was to partition India? Whatever the shortcomings of apartheid, and they were probably many, the best way to deal with them seemed to be to work towards their rectification.

I remember that about that time Dr Verwoerd was appointed Minister of Native Affairs and one of his first public pronouncements was: 'We are not oppressors; we know only too well what it is to be oppressed.' In the frame of mind that I was in then, that

24

statement was very impressive. It struck just the right chord in me at just the right time.

Strangely enough, my acceptance of the apartheid ideal as the best solution of the country's problems allowed a fuller development of my interest in and attachment to both peoples. Otherwise, I might have felt obliged to choose between one or the other.

But my changing attitude towards Africans, the fact that I saw them as flesh and blood, found no outward expression. I did not seek African company. I did not even speak about it, except to Daan van Tonder. Not until several months after I had resigned from the Foreign Service did I come to know any African at all well. My conversion was a change within myself.

It was obvious that I now had to deal somehow with my personal dislike of Indians; it could not be maintained in isolation. In the course of my work I had a great deal of contact with estate agents, lawyers and accountants. One of the people that I met was an Indian named P. R. Pather. He was fairly prominent in Indian political circles in Durban, and he had reason to call and see me in the office about the estate of a deceased person. He was a large man who looked very much like a darker version of J. H. Hofmeyr, one of the liberals in the Smuts Government. This was the first time I had ever sat down with an Indian, and because I was very conscious of it, I was, if anything, over-courteous. He behaved quite normally and he set me at my ease. When he left, I didn't think that he had grasped the problem we had been discussing; he doubtless felt that I hadn't. But he had helped me over a first, very real hurdle. As atonement for my previous attitude, I was thereafter particularly painstaking and helpful to an Indian charitable society which assisted poorer Indian families to wind up the estates of their deceased relatives. Up till then I had always been rather brusque with them.

At the end of 1952, just before I completed my degree, I applied for a transfer to the Department of External Affairs. I was not really happy in the work that I was doing. I was taking a wider interest in world affairs, and the prospect of going abroad as a diplomat attracted me. I felt that the work would be more 'vital'. In March 1953, I was appointed as a cadet diplomat and transferred to Pretoria. I was assigned to the political division, where I stayed for three years.

In many respects I had already become a confirmed civil servant, and this in the space of four years. The service, with its claim to offer 'security', deceives one into comparative contentment with salaries lower than can be earned elsewhere. There is a pension. Instances of dismissal are almost unknown. My gross salary, in the middle of 1949, had been fifteen pounds per month, plus two pounds ten shillings cost-of-living allowance. My studies alone cost me over five pounds per month, which meant, in the end, that there was little I could afford to do except study. I found relaxation in sport — and did tolerably well. I played for the Natal provincial under-nineteen Rugby team, and became, at twenty-one, an umpire in a first-class cricket match.

In the civil service one has a vague 'sense of service', which, like the 'sense of security', is much vaunted in the advertisements of vacant posts. If by this time I had begun privately thinking of Africans and Indians as people, I had already been a civil servant too long to imagine that I had any responsibility to communicate this purely personal feeling. I had no other duty than to serve the government of the day with loyalty and to the best of my ability.

The conviction that the apartheid ideal was the only possible, if not the perfect, solution for South Africa was strengthened in me. At the United Nations South Africa was coming under increasingly heavy fire, and the division of the Department of External Affairs in which I worked was concerned, among other things, with our relations with the United Nations. I was responsible for compiling a document which was jokingly referred to as 'The Case Against India', which I intended to be an indictment against India on many of the charges which she levelled at South Africa. She was at that time the prime accuser of the Union. The suggestion of compiling this document had been my own. For all I know it may well still be in use.

(In passing, I may say that Mr Krishna Menon made the best answer I have yet seen to this kind of 'You too' reply to criticism, when, during the 1960 session of the United Nations General Assembly, he pleaded guilty to various manifestations of prejudice in his own country and elsewhere, but pointed out that only in South Africa was prejudice given the force of law. Elsewhere law was arraigned against it. At the time, however, I was angered by Indian attacks on South Africa, many of which were ill-informed.)

In my work, at this time, I became more closely acquainted with the arguments in favour of apartheid and had more information about its practical implementation. My division of the Department of External Affairs was the channel between the Ministries responsible for putting it into effect and our speech-makers at the United Nations. We also linked the Ministries with our professional apologists abroad. The basic and essential case for apartheid was the one that persuaded me: that the only manner of reconciling the head-on conflict between Boer and African lay in separation. But it was not the shortcomings in policy that were being attacked abroad, but the policy itself. It was called impractical and unethical; yet among our critics were Indians and Pakistanis who were the living testimony of partition.

Within South Africa, voices were being raised against the long delays in doing anything practical about separation; some people were becoming critical of the Government's methods. They said that separation should not be imposed, but agreed on by all who were affected; that the Government alone should not decide the extent of the land that was to be shared, but that that too should be agreed on. It was 1954, and the Government had been in power for six years.

In my view, the impatient voices alone among the Government's critics had a case. My own uneasiness began to grow. But what could I do about it? In 1955, through some of my colleagues, I made contact with several leading members of the Nasionale Jeugbond, the youth organization of the Afrikaner National Party, and attended one or two of their discussion groups. I found the same uneasiness and impatience among a few of these young men. I was to meet them again, much later, with important consequences.

I felt that although our policy was the only one possible it was not sufficient so long as it remained on paper only. Yet the longer I stayed in government service, the less likely I was to voice criticism of official policy aloud. The work of a young diplomat is fascinating and offers pleasing prospects, and I hoped to do well. I tried to smother my uneasy conscience, *not* to think about matters which disturbed it.

It seemed to me during those years that men like me who might have been critical of aspects of government policy were perhaps more conscientious in their application of it than those who were blindly loyal. Certainly I can say that in whatever respect I might then have disagreed with government policies — and even later when the disagreement became wider — I gave of my best. I have never since betrayed any one of the official secrets in my possession, either deliberately or accidentally. Indeed, I am constantly on guard against doing so. They were entrusted to me while I was a paid employee of the state, and I believe it would be a breach of good faith to use knowledge so acquired in my fight against the Government, however bitter a fight it may be.

In February 1956 I was sent to Leopoldville as the South African Vice-Consul. I was twenty-four years old, and it was the first time that I had ever been outside South Africa. My numerous duties included writing political reports on the Congo. It was a time of great change in the colony. Political consciousness was emerging in an articulate form. The Congo had until then been the 'one oasis of peace in a turbulent Africa', as the Belgians chose to describe it. By studying the affairs of the Congo from near at hand I gained for the first time a proper knowledge of a policy in Africa other than the Union's. I also learned something about the rise of African nationalism.

There were some apparent points in apartheid's favour to be drawn from the comparison. The Belgians had set out to avoid the development of a White working class whose interests would conflict with those of the Congolese. They were also conscious of the effect on the Congolese of widespread racial discrimination. They kept their working class in Belgium and did what they could to minimize the inevitable racial prejudices of the Whites. In South Africa, we already had a conflict between the interests of Black and White workers, but we had no home base in Europe to which the Whites could go. The answer clearly lay in territorial separation. When I wrote thus in my reports, I did not do so just as an analysis of the situation. It was an attempt in a very small way to remind someone at home, big or small, that this *was* the official policy.

It was now eight years since the Government had come to power. Dr Malan had given way to Mr Strijdom, Parliament each year had a packed and heavy legislative programme, but hardly any advance had been made towards a real attempt at physical separation. The outside world was beginning to focus its attention on the legislative programme, which included a number of very contentious measures. All we could say was that these were a necessary prelude to total territorial separation. Some of my closer foreign friends in the consular corps were very critical, in our private discussions, of trends in the Union. I could make only a sketchy attempt to convince them by painting the broad picture of the Union, with its variegated population at very different levels of development. The Government's first duty was to eliminate poverty and unemployment among the Whites in the White areas, and to do this would inevitably entail hardships for some non-Whites. Total territorial separation was a costly business, and if all the Blacks were suddenly moved out of the White areas, the labour force would be cut off and industry brought to an immediate standstill. Furthermore, many Whites had to be educated into accepting the consequences of separation. They would be without servants, and the urban labour force would have to be provided from among the Whites. To many this might not be a pleasing prospect. In our endless arguments some of my friends showed a better grasp of the situation than I expected. I knew just that much more than they did for me to score a temporary point, perhaps. But my own answers left me unconvinced.

The truth was that apartheid was assuming a form different from that in which I had idealized it. It was no longer allowing me to reconcile my sympathy for both Afrikaner and African as people. The Government had launched a frontal attack on the human rights of Africans, and I was only now becoming properly aware of it — largely through the criticisms of my friends. I was being forced to choose between my sympathies. The Nationalists were doing absolutely nothing about territorial separation. There were many signs that the Africans were reacting powerfully to Government policies, and that their militancy and determination were growing. The Afrikaner Nationalists had always claimed that there was no middle course; that they must dominate or be dominated. They were proving themselves correct or being proved so — depending on the way one looked at it.

After that I stopped thinking about apartheid. It was not my job to make the decisions. I began to enjoy myself in Leopoldville. I had many friends now. I was young, and there were all the years ahead in which to worry about problems like this. In any case, the world was beset by problems about which I could do absolutely nothing. I liked my job and I liked the advantages that went with it.

Towards the end of 1956 and early in 1957 a number of things happened in quick succession. A hundred and fifty-six people were arrested on charges of high treason. The Bantu Education Act was passed, and the Minister of Native Affairs virtually admitted that its objective was to provide inferior education for Africans. A plan to do the same at university level was officially announced, and Government spokesmen declared that African parliamentary representation would be abolished. It was also the year of the 'church clause'. (This familiarly describes the section of an Act passed in early 1957, giving the Minister of Native Affairs the power to prohibit worship together of Black and White. In

other sections, the Minister was given authority to outlaw racial
mixing at various kinds of meetings and at social functions.)

This happened at the very time that I was making my first
social contacts with Africans. These were admittedly limited contacts, and I had rather ostentatiously gone out of my way at a few
receptions to find some of the Africans present. (It hadn't, after
all, been a shock when we shook hands.) At one reception, I had
a long conversation with a man who later became mayor of one
of the Congo towns. When I saw him again, at another reception,
I noticed the Czech consul talking at length to him. I intruded,
and immediately brought the conversation down to trivialities;
then I adopted him for the rest of the party, since I felt I had a
duty to 'protect' him from subversion! I didn't realize it then because it had happened surreptitiously, but yet another barrier had
gone. And it went just as Parliament in the Union passed an Act
designed to build the barriers higher.

One of my close friends was a thirty-two-year-old Australian,
Roger M——, an engineer whose job it was to ensure that the
U.S. Consulate-General was properly built. He was then a rolling
stone, a sower of wild oats (to the despair of his mother), and a
man about town — both towns. For as everywhere in colonized
Africa, Leopoldville was really two towns, one Black, one White.
Roger moved with equal ease and enjoyment in either. He could
never understand why I kept so exclusively to White Leopoldville,
and tried often to tell me what I was missing. His work had taken
him to Nigeria and Ethiopia, and his stories, films, trophies and
souvenirs were fascinating. Without trying to, he showed me a life
in Africa of which I knew nothing, despite the fact that I had
never set foot outside the continent. When I arrived in Leopoldville, I was young enough to have judged its attractions simply by
the number of young White girls I saw about me. He felt I was
missing a great deal.

He didn't set out to break down my prejudices. More often than
not, when he spoke of his experiences and journeys, he went
happily on as if he were speaking to someone whom he thought

felt precisely as he did, and would envy the things he had done — spending a night in an African home in the wild country during a tour of Ethiopia, or dancing in a colour-blind night club in Lagos. It didn't matter what it was — his pleasure was always infectious.

I had been close enough to Afrikaner nationalism to realize the power of its emotional grip, without ever having been completely gripped by it. If one believes in something intellectually, there must come an emotional involvement. It is a terrible thing to live with your heart in one place and your mind in another. My background was emotionally complex; my childhood memories were of something different from Afrikanerdom, and my first passion for Afrikaners was a passion for misunderstood and maligned *people*. My memories of my intimate association with Afrikaners were fond ones; my attachment to Afrikanerdom was strong, not overpowering. If it had been stronger, it would probably have stifled the critical thoughts inside me; for I had begun by this time to have very serious doubts about the Government's good faith in applying territorial separation. I began to wonder whether this declared policy were not, in fact, a hoax and a cover-up for something quite different. This was certainly being suggested by numerous critics at home, and in books by commentators like the Dutch Calvinist, Dr J. J. Buskes, and the Swedish editor, Professor H. H. Tingsten.

During the following weeks I made a point of going through some of the volumes of the South African Acts of Parliament which we had in our office library. After that, I leafed through Hansard. I made notes of the contents of various sections of Acts, and on various points in speeches by Nationalist Cabinet Ministers. (I still have these notes, and have used some later in this book to substantiate and document discussions of Government policy.)

I was shocked by many of the discoveries I made. So much of the detail of many of the Acts and of many speeches by leading members of the Government had not been published, either because the papers were too full when the matter was reported, or perhaps because they made dull reading. There was certainly a great deal that was new to me; enough to make it seem highly probable that the Government had some motive other than territorial separation. It wanted the African away, but it also wanted his labour. If he remained among them, the Whites could be secure only if they were completely on top of him. It was clear that the Government was doing precisely that: getting on top of him. They were convinced from their history that there was no chance of sharing power, so they would either be on top or they would be under. The more they set out to put themselves on top, the more probable did it become that if the Africans could ever break through, they would do to the Afrikaners precisely what the Afrikaners anticipated. They had therefore to ensure that there would be no break-through. They knew how to do this perhaps better than others, because it was precisely what the British had done to them. What they were doing in their relations with the Africans was wrong, and at last I was convinced of it.

I emerged from those long nights of note-taking disappointed and disillusioned. It was clear now that the choice had to be between the two peoples. There was no longer a way out.

In effect, I had already chosen. I was a part of the machinery of one against the other, a very small part perhaps, a tiny cog in a big wheel. I could say that as a civil servant I was not in effect making any choice, but simply carrying out the policy of the government of the day. That would have been truer if I had still been in the Office of the Master of the Supreme Court, dealing only with technical matters; but it was infinitely less true now. The Government was developing its Africa policy. It wanted to establish friendship with the African independent states so that it might be allowed to work out its own policies in the Union with the minimum of attack from them. I was a tool of that policy so long as I remained in the Congo, and I was contributing in some measure to the oppression of one section by the other. It may have been infinitesimal in measure, but it concerned me very deeply.

Had Afrikanerdom been an essential part of me emotionally, I should probably have felt bound to choose it. Otherwise I should have been required to sacrifice a whole way of life. When I did eventually resign, the Consul-General seemed genuinely upset, but when I told him the reason — that it was because of apartheid — he understood immediately. He knew as well as I did that one was required to make a choice between peoples, and he had made his. Afrikanerdom was essentially a part of him. He said that when he was a child, his mother had told him the stories and sung him the songs of the Boer War. What he did not say (but it was quite clear) was that for him a break for intellectual reasons would have meant the destruction of his world. It would have been a break from the religion of a lifetime, from friends, loved ones, a tradition, a history, a way of life. As he talked, I felt for a moment sad that I had missed the childhood memories. Perhaps it was as well.

Ghana had become independent in March 1957, and was to me a vague symbol of the upsurge of the African people. I was anxious to know how they would manage their affairs; anxious, even then, to see them succeed. I was beginning to feel unhappy at the thought that I was associated with the machinery of domination of Africans. I didn't necessarily want to choose against the Afrikaner, but I was conscious that I had unwittingly chosen against the African. I had a *vague* feeling that I should resign.

But it was easier said than done. It was not just a matter of abandoning a job that I had grown to like and which offered pleasant prospects. It was also a question of giving up the security that I had become used to. What else was I to do? I felt diffident· at the thought of making my way in the unaccustomed outside world, away from the shelter of the one I knew. Had I waited and been transferred to a European post, I might have postponed a decision indefinitely. I had come to a conclusion about the politics of my position, but I had not the courage to see it through at once. Though, therefore, the decision had been made some while before, when I acted I did so impulsively. Perhaps I would never have done it otherwise.

I had been spending the early part of the evening with a few close friends, including Roger M———. We had discussed South Africa critically. I went home with Roger, and he suggested that we stop at a fair which was being held in the town. We did so; there was nothing better to do. I kept my distance a little as Roger mingled freely with everybody, and they were mostly Congolese there. Roger danced with the darker girls and thoroughly enjoyed himself. He made me feel I was missing something. We left after a while and went to his flat, where we chatted and listened to music.

I picked up one of the books from his bookshelf. It was Chester Bowles's *Africa's Challenge to America* and I glanced through it.

'Can I borrow this?'

'Of course.'

I think that book had a greater impact on me than anything I had read before, and at a moment when I was most receptive. I was half-way through it before I left Roger's flat. At some point I looked up from the book and told him I was going to resign.

'I've thought for some time that you would,' he said. 'You should get it over.'

He said nothing more, and I remember he went out of the room for something — perhaps to the kitchen and the fridge to get another beer. I remember very few details, only that we didn't mention it again. I cannot even remember precisely what it was that made me say that I was going to resign.

I took the book home and finished it.

Chester Bowles had found racialism in many parts of the world, he said, but only in Germany under Hitler and in South Africa was it incorporated as a principle of government. In South Africa it was one of the cardinal principles of state policy. He put all that into one sentence. In South Africa, racial prejudice was 'sanctified by religion and philosophy, formalized by law and institutionalized in the mores of the nation'. He said no more than liberals all over the world were saying, but to me that evening he said it cogently, tersely and meaningfully. He admitted the choice in South Africa might be between two peoples and between two forces of the same kind standing for two different races — but that was only because there were not enough liberals, and not enough liberalism.

There were a thousand questions and problems that stemmed from all this, and it has taken me a long time to sort out my views; the sorting out has perhaps not ended, even now. But my active participation in politics has made things clearer to me, and has brought the answers to some of the questons that arose only as I faced them.

When I awoke the following morning, the first thought in my mind was that I had decided to resign. I had said so aloud. I wondered if I ought to think it over, or at least discuss it with someone, but I knew I wouldn't. I had to get on with it, even if I was going to regret it afterwards. I was at the office earlier that morning than I had ever been. I wanted to tell the Consul-General right away, so that there could be no going back. Since then, I have sometimes thought wistfully about the job, but I have never regretted the decision.

Immediately after my resignation I felt a strange sense of relief. I wanted to be away as soon as possible. Having told the Consul-General of my decision, I confirmed it in writing. I said that I 'no longer felt conscientiously able to defend the policies of the Union Government', and that if I remained I should be disloyal either to my conscience or to my employers, and I would be neither. Resignation was the only honest course open to me.

My resignation was accepted without comment and my services were to terminate on May 31st, 1957. The Consul-General, in sending my letter of resignation to the Department of External Affairs, had, so far as I was concerned, said the nicest thing possible in his covering letter, namely, that as far as he had seen I had been completely loyal to the Government at all times. I am glad that was so.

My last official duty was to attend the reception on Union Day — South Africa's national day, May 31st. I did not suggest to anyone that it was my farewell party, although I was tempted to do so. The following day I was among the unemployed.

When I returned to the Union on June 7th, it was to find that the South African press had taken some interest in my resignation. There were a few reporters and photographers at the Jan Smuts Airport. I was quite unprepared for this, and I was a little scared of attracting attention. I made no statements or comments. I was not sure that press comment would be sympathetic. Some people might resent quite strongly what I had done.

I had first to find a job. I had a little difficulty, but after about eleven days I was given employment as a trainee executive with a firm of tobacco wholesalers in Johannesburg. During the next four or five months I took no part in any political activity, except that immediately after my return to the Union I wrote three newspaper articles on South Africa's position in Africa and in relation to the United Nations.

I was aware of certain pitfalls to be avoided. For instance, I had to avoid the tendency (in reaction) to become a Negrophil with an inverted sense of race prejudice. It was not a danger I then felt prone to, but in a situation in which one race oppresses another, for whatever reason, there is always the danger that a liberal may identify himself wholly with the oppressed. I was, I suppose, already a liberal — with a small 'l'.

There was much to be thought out. Was my resignation to be a gesture that in itself would achieve no more than the satisfaction of my own conscience? Or was I to engage in political activity? If so, in which movement and to what end? If I was to do absolutely nothing in the way of politics, then I would simply return home to enjoy the benefits of the system of White domination that we had all constructed, secure in the knowledge that my guilt had been absolved by my resignation from the Foreign Service. What I had really hoped to see in South Africa was a country in which there were the same opportunities for people of all races, but that hope had a vast ramification in terms of a practical policy,

GUILTY LAND

and I had to face all this. What did I think of votes for all? What was the state of African opinion? What I had seen of it seemed favourable to multi-racialism, but how representative was that? Again, could we really change the Government by internal means alone? It did not seem to me possible at the time. Was I then in favour of looking for aid abroad? I was not completely sure.

And if after a time, I felt that multi-racialism was not possible, that the policy of humanity or 'people count' had failed because African nationalism had become anti-White, what then? I should simply have facilitated the downfall of the Afrikaner by becoming an ally of an embittered African nationalism and fighting against White Afrikaner nationalism. My intention might well have been to create a third force, but I should have failed.

These were the kinds of questions that confronted me. Even now, when I think I may have answered them, I have doubts. I have devoted a large part of this book to some of these questions but their very answers pose new problems.

At first I thought of joining the United Party because it seemed at least to have a chance of ousting the Government. Then, in November 1957, I met Patrick Duncan for the first time. He was the Liberal Party's national organizer, and over lunch we discussed the political situation. I had previously met a young member of the Liberal Party's Transvaal executive, Wolf Hamm, who subsequently became a close friend. He had devoted much time to persuading me to join the Liberal Party. Pat Duncan finally convinced me to do so, and also invited me to be a sponsor of the Multi-Racial Conference opening in December, 1957.

I made my first public speech at the Liberal Party's national conference in Durban later in the same month. As a former member of the Department of External Affairs, I replied to an attack which had been made by Mr Eric Louw, the Minister, on prominent people (including some of our party leaders) who had signed a declaration on Human Rights in South Africa. I was extremely nervous. I think my hands must have trembled noticeably when I spoke. But in many senses I had taken the plunge.

A TRAITOR TO HATRED

And during the months following I became active in Liberal Party politics.

Early in 1958 I met three of the accused men in the Treason Trial. Two were Africans and the other man was Coloured (a Eurafrican). They were Robert Resha, Jonas (Joe) Matlou and Stanley Lollan — now three of my closest friends. I owe them a lot, not for what they did consciously, but because they were always themselves and I learned to know them as people rather than as members of an oppressed racial group. Through them, I made many new friends — African, Indian, Coloured and White. Not that they introduced me to a 'new world', but they allowed me to see more clearly what had been wrong with me.

I saw much of them, but we could not go out together to many places. In South Africa, hotels, bars, cinemas, plays, concerts, night clubs, dances and restaurants are for Whites only. Everything else is segregated, with seats for Whites and separate seats for Blacks, so that we were continually reminded of our racial differences. But we learned to meet in our own homes, adapting ourselves in that way to the difficult world around us, and constantly forgetting it until it intruded again, sometimes forcibly. Because even their township homes gave us no privacy. Robert and Joe were then living in Sophiatown — the only township for which Whites needed no entry permit. Even so, two or three times a roving police car spotted me entering or leaving the house of one or other of them. To the police, a White man's purpose in a township could only be illegal or subversive. If we met in the streets and stopped to chat — which happened often — we occasionally attracted hostile attention. But only occasionally.

One evening I was visiting some friends in Sophiatown whom I had met through Robert. He was not there that evening, nor were Stanley and Joe. A few other Whites had joined us that night. The trouble started just as we were leaving. I was giving some of the guests a lift, and as I was starting to drive off, one of them remembered something he had left inside. He went to fetch it, and while we were waiting for him a police car drew up and stopped in front of mine. One carload of guests was already pulling away, but they stopped when they saw the police car — the 'scorpion'.

The police constable who came to speak to me was quite friendly. What was I doing there? I told him I was visiting friends. '*Ongelooflik* (incredible),' he said. 'A White man with "kaffir" friends?' He was most upset. There was real pain in his face. I told him that it was the thing nowadays; the Nationalist Bureau of Racial Affairs (SABRA) was planning to meet African leaders. He said he hadn't heard of it. He came from a little country town where such things did not happen.

His colleague had already quietly slipped into V——'s house. He had a less pleasant face. He came out leading V——'s wife J—— by the arm. She was carrying a tray with nine empty glasses. They were the evidence, since it was then a criminal offence in the Union for any White man to serve liquor to *any* African, and an offence for Africans to have it in their possession without a valid permit. Had I supplied liquor? No. Who had? I was not prepared to say. We set off, two carloads of us (V—— and his wife in the police car), for Marshall Square, the police headquarters. On the way the scorpion stopped. The more friendly constable came back and said that we and the passengers in the other car could go home. By then I didn't want to. None of us did. So we followed the police car to the Newlands police-station.

There must have been eleven of us rolling into the charge office that evening. We were, I think, in a provocative mood, feeling that *we* had been provoked. V——'s wife was being charged with unlawful possession of 'European' liquor. We were all ready to spend the night there unless the silly charge against her was withdrawn. In the end bail was arranged and she was allowed to go home. (The next day the prosecutor dropped the charge.)

We ignored all apartheid regulations at the police station that night. At one moment we were all in the African section of the charge office, in the next all in the White. The police said that those who had been told to go should do so. We stayed, and 'borrowed' cigarettes from African policemen. Someone even asked one of them for a drink. We all laughed, including the policeman. Cigarettes were short and an African ended up by sharing one with the young girl who had accompanied me. A policeman leered at us from the dark entrance to the charge office. As the African passed the cigarette to the girl after his puff, the policeman lunged forward and struck it out of her hand. We all gathered round him. We had to remember that face. We would have to be able to identify him later if we laid an assault charge. 'Take off your cap,' I said to him. He pulled it down further on his head. He was livid, but he said nothing. We had all laughed a lot that evening, but it was over now.

When Robert, Stanley, Joe and I were together, we talked about many things, and naturally we often spoke of politics. Unquestionably they influenced my political thinking and undermined some of my firmest beliefs. They caused me to doubt the justice of the 'qualified franchise', and when I passed from the world we shared to the White world they did not share, I realized how great was the gulf between men in our land. I learned of their dreams and aspirations — which struck me as natural and human — yet moved from them to the shining White world of office desks and pink faces, the reserved world of bar saloons and red faces, where the old, old view that the Black man was inferior remained.

Logic carried no weight with the Whites; they were digging their gold from the side of a volcano, and until it erupted they would not stop, not even to think. From personal experience I was learning that those of us who warned about the volcano were accused of creating it.

In the middle of 1958 I was able to bring my African friends together with a number of young Afrikaners, some of whom, former Young Nationalists (Jeugbonders), were now leading members of the Pretoria Political Study Group. I had met these young men earlier when I was in the Department of External Affairs, and later I joined this political study group. Once a month the group invited prominent South Africans of all political persuasions to address it, and its main function was the study of the country's political problems. As a result of discussions between these young Afrikaners and the Africans, the way was cleared for ex-Chief A. J. Luthuli, President General of the African National Congress, to address the group. He did so at one of its best attended meetings, but it was a tragic evening. He and the chairman were assaulted by a gang of thugs, and the news of the brawl echoed half-way round the world.

In September 1958 I accepted a post as organizing secretary of the Liberal Party in the Transvaal, a post I intended to hold for about nine months before going abroad. At this time the Party was expanding considerably and beginning to enjoy a greatly increased publicity. During this period I was twice threatened with assault by the special police while attending meetings. I complained to the Minister of Justice about these incidents, but his reply never reached me. In fairness, I must admit that the conduct of most of these special branch men was unfailingly correct. The threats against me were not due to the fact that I was particularly dangerous or subversive, but simply to the fact that I bore an Afrikaans name. That meant that I had 'deserted' my people, and magnified even the little that I had done. I cannot hide the fact that these threats disturbed me, because I abhor physical violence. Nevertheless, I continued with my work simply because I knew that many other people were far more vulnerable than I, yet never shirked their duties. Everything in South Africa favours the Whites, and the system by and large protects even the 'bad' Whites; though I may be a traitor, I am White, and consequently the caste system will always rate me higher than a Black. An assault on me will be news, whereas assaults on Africans seldom make the headlines. In the townships the police can often act in the shadows of public unconcern.

Soon after I gave up my job as Liberal Party organizing secretary the Government served a notice on ex-Chief Luthuli under the Suppression of Communism Act, confining him for five years to the magisterial area of Groutville, Natal, and prohibiting him from addressing or attending any meetings during that period. I suggested to the Liberal Party executive that we should seek permission to hold a meeting of protest on the Johannesburg City Hall steps. Surprisingly enough, permission was granted by the City Council.

More than three thousand people attended our meeting — one of the biggest we had ever had. It was addressed by the chairman of the Party in the Transvaal, Mr Jack Unterhalter; a former city councillor, Mr Jack Lewsen; and me. The City Hall was ringed with police that day — two hundred of them, according to press reports. They had recommended to the Council that the meeting be cancelled. I recognized a number of special policemen there, including the head of the special branch from Pretoria. I said in my speech that there were a number of parallels between the Pretoria assault on Chief Luthuli and his present banning. In both cases an attempt was made to silence the President of the African National Congress; though he spoke with moderation and warned against sectional nationalism in a multi-racial country, neither his assailants that night at Pretoria, nor the Government in this act of banning and banishment, paid any heed to his language. He was black and he was to be silenced. He could say nothing unless it was to praise the white man. The hooligans who had kicked him in the face would be happy to know that the Government was continuing their own attempts to silence Mr Luthuli with an act of political hooliganism. Chief Luthuli came out of the assault without rancour, and with no hate for the white man; he reacted with the same moderation to the banning.

Shortly after that I booked a sea passage to Britain, as I had already decided that I would like to see Europe. I left surreptitiously, because I was afraid that if I did so openly I might draw attention to the fact that I possessed a passport. I was sure that the authorities did not realize that I had one, although the information was certainly on record. I very much wanted to make my first visit to Europe, and while I did not think it probable that

my passport would be seized, I wanted to guard against the re-
motest possibility.

I arrived in London fairly broke. In Leopoldville I had received
a totally inadequate salary as my country's representative in a
place with a high cost of living. Moreover, the Union Government
— as is its custom in cases of resignation—paid neither my passage
back to South Africa, nor the costs of transport of my car and
possessions. The money I had to find constituted something of a
burden for months afterwards, because on my even smaller salary
in South Africa I was discharging the debt of an infinitely more
expensive life — a debt incurred in my country's service.

Within two days of arriving in London I took a job as a
'griddler', making hamburgers in a Corner House on the Strand—
opposite South Africa House. One of the customers during my
five weeks there was a former colleague in the Foreign Service.
Then I met Canon L. John Collins, and he invited me to help
him raise money for the Defence and Aid Fund, administered
by Christian Action. The fund assists persecuted people in South
Africa.

Soon afterwards I ran into Tennyson Makiwane again, one of
Robert Resha's friends. We had seen a fair amount of each other
at home. He discussed with me the boycott of South African goods
which he had launched before my arrival, and asked me to help
him. I told him I would think seriously about it. I thought it over
for six weeks, and then decided to assist. I at once wrote to Peter
Brown, National Chairman of the Liberal Party, telling him that
I would do so on certain conditions, the chief of which was that it
should be a limited campaign with limited objectives. He supported my decision and gave me a full go-ahead. I respected Peter
Brown immensely, and had been almost certain that he would
endorse this action; my main problem, as usual, was a personal
one. I was doing something I knew must have dangerous personal
implications for one who intended returning to South Africa.

By now, the original campaign had virtually petered out. I
suggested to Tennyson that we wait until the British general elec-

tion and the post-mortems were over, before raising the matter again. When we did so, it quickly gained ground. Tennyson had readily accepted the suggestion that the campaign should be of limited duration. In any case, if it was to continue, it would do so only if it had an initial impetus; it would not get that if responsible backing were absent; and it was clear that this would not be given to an indefinite campaign. The campaign already launched had shown this. From then on Tennyson and I worked closely together, and a Boycott Movement came into being.

During November 1959 I travelled to Holland, where a lecture tour had been arranged for me by Dr Karel Roskam in association with Dr J. J. Buskes. I had met Dr Roskam in South Africa, where he had been studying for a year. I spent two weeks in Holland, addressing meetings in Afrikaans. Towards the end of my stay the South African Ambassador issued a statement vigorously denying various of my charges against the Government. *Die Burger*, the Cape Nationalist Afrikaans-language newspaper, devoted a leading article to an attack on me and the Liberal Party a few days later. It was entitled 'Distant Fighters'.

On January 17th, 1960, I left London, satisfied that the boycott had had as good a send-off as possible, and relinquishing the directorate of the Boycott Movement. I was on my way to Tunis to represent the Liberal Party at the All-African People's Conference. Before I left, the South African Liberal Party had told me by telephone that feeling was running high against me in the Union because of my share in the boycott campaign. They warned me not to return at that moment. From letters I received later, it seemed that my attendance at the Tunis Conference provoked a new outburst against me, particularly in the Government press. Acting on this advice, I postponed my return to the Union.

I was well received at the Tunis Conference as the first White African ever to speak at a public session as a full member. I regarded this as a recognition of the anti-racialism of the new Africa, in which Africans could be White and Whites could be African.

Having decided to postpone my return home, I travelled to

Accra, where I spent six weeks. From such newspapers as I was able to see, and from the few letters I had from South Africa, it was clear that the attacks on me in the South African press continued sporadically throughout February. At the beginning of March, the boycott month, they increased, and the Johannesburg *Sunday Times* for February 28th stated in a leading article on their front page that the Government planned to introduce legislation to make it an offence to advocate boycott, at home or abroad. I was reported to have 'incensed Nationalist M.P.s', who were demanding that I should be banned from all political activity and my passport seized. There must have been several suggestions of violence against me, too, serious enough for the columnist of *Die Burger* to warn that 'if a hair of his head is harmed' it could only further the cause I had taken up.

Die Vaderland, commenting on January 9th, 1960, on my post at a Johannesburg school, said that the question had been raised 'whether this person should be allowed to return to the country to which he wanted to do so much harm. Politicians recall how the English-language press at the time made such a fuss about Mr Derek Alexander, the "lieutenant" of the British Fascist leader, Sir Oswald Mosley, in South Africa. The agitation was so severe that Mr Alexander was removed from his teaching post at the Twist Street School. This, however, is a government school.'

On January 11th, 1960, the same paper asked whether it was not time for legislation against boycotts. 'Or is it just what the political snake-people and groups desire in order to pose as martyrs to their fellow-spirits here and overseas? Whatever the case may be, it is almost unthinkable that any civilized country would permit one of its citizens, like the arch-Liberalist Patrick van Rensburg, to associate himself actively with the boycott movement and then calmly and with impunity return to his fatherland which he tried so flagrantly to stab in the back.'

In mid-February it was reported that the Department of the Interior proposed to the Minister of External Affairs that I be declared a stateless person. Mr Louw turned down this unusual and ingenious proposal on the grounds that it would only add fuel to the fire we had lighted.

I had been away from South Africa about a year, and wanted desperately to be home again, although I was enjoying my stay in Accra with an old friend from the Johannesburg townships, Alfred Hutchinson. While there, I wrote a number of articles, addressed a couple of meetings, and called on many people in an attempt to spread the boycott. I also received news that my flat in Johannesburg had been searched from top to bottom by the special police. I was desperately afraid of what would happen when I returned. From Accra I went to Leopoldville, where I renewed old acquaintances; then to Livingstone, and on to Bulawayo to wait and watch from close by.

While I was in Leopoldville, Sharpeville happened. I spent two days beside a ticker tape in a news agency office, reading thousands of words about the massacre and the reactions of a horrified world. I thought then of all the people I knew and loved in the townships. I was more than ever determined to return home to be with my friends again.

Sharpeville meant that South Africa would now be preoccupied with far more important things than wreaking vengeance on Patrick van Rensburg. I flew to Johannesburg on March 28th, still afraid. It was the day of mourning for the Sharpeville martyrs; Africans had been asked by their leaders to stay at home. All the special policemen would be out in the townships. I knew that the flight was too short for the passenger list to be signalled ahead, and I reasoned that there would be no time to send for any special policemen, even if they could be spared. Using a pre-arranged code, I telegraphed to a lawyer, asking him to meet me at the airport. Then I had a few beers to steady my nerves. When we landed I saw two khaki-clad policemen at the Jan Smuts Airport, and knew I was home again. Two policemen always come out to meet the aircraft, but I was no less afraid for knowing that. They remained impassive while the passengers alighted and filed through to the waiting-room, to be called by the immigration and customs officers. I was the last through. It was a long wait, and I knew that something was going to happen. The immigration officer very courteously took my passport away from me; the customs officers were all watching me as one of them searched my bag. Then the chief officer said that a lawyer was waiting for me. I felt a great deal better.

The Nationalist Afrikaans-language paper *Die Vaderland,* which is published in Johannesburg, carried a front page report: '*Patrick van Rensburg Iewers in Goudstad*'. I was 'somewhere in the Golden City'. I thought that it was perhaps a signal to the thugs, and it confirmed my decision to stay in hiding for a while. During the next two days there was nothing more in the papers about my return. There were, I thought, bigger things to worry about after Sharpeville.

On the morning of March 30th I awoke to hear that a vast number of people had been arrested throughout the country. The Emergency had been proclaimed. Eleven of my colleagues from the Liberal Party were detained. (There were more later.) Perhaps I should not have returned at this moment, after all. I had certainly never anticipated this. Nevertheless, I decided I ought to come out into the open, but my colleagues thought differently. They thought that those not in the hands of the police should stay that way; I was to go to Swaziland, from where I might, if necessary and if possible, go abroad again.

We left Johannesburg at midnight, and on the way through Pretoria we passed forty or fifty military trucks rolling on to Johannesburg, but we did not slow down to see what was inside them. It was an anxious journey. The driver had been to Swaziland once before and remembered that there was a police post near the border, where, very occasionally, motorists were stopped. Would they stop us? Our anxiety increased as we approached the border, but we were not stopped. We did the two hundred and twenty miles in five hours, halting to drink the tea and eat the sandwiches we had brought with us only when we were well across the border. I had not wanted to be on the run, and now that I was, I was anxious and a little afraid. So was the driver, who was not himself in politics.

In Mbabane, Swaziland, I found a man who had already preceded me. He was a young actor who had been arrested in the pre-dawn swoops of that morning and released when the Supreme Court found that the Emergency had not been properly proclaimed. We were the first of the 'refugees'. Others had also been able to flee; arrested and released, they disappeared before they could be re-arrested. Others again had been warned of the arrests and had fled. But in spite of all the police blunders, these were only a fraction of those eventually arrested and held. There was no pattern to the arrests; dozens of people were picked up who had not been politically active for years, simply because, ten or twenty years earlier, they had been members of the outlawed Communist Party. Those who got away could thank the inefficiency of the police — the only quality that now mitigates tyranny in our country.

I had been in Swaziland for several days when newspaper reporters, seeking an interview with the Bishop of Johannesburg, who was also there, discovered my name in an hotel register. My whereabouts were quickly published in the press. Earlier, on the night of April 2nd, the special police had called on Wolf Hamm: they knew that we were close friends, that we had been in correspondence, and that I would see him on my return to Johannesburg. They probably knew what had been in our letters, and they now wanted to know from him where I was.

He wrote to me as follows about the visit he had had from the special police:

Then on Monday evening my boss came to see me, because he thought it possible that Celeste's [his wife's] phone call in the morning telling him that I was ill was a cover-up for detention [under the Emergency]. While he was sitting there with his wife, Celeste, and myself, the door-bell rang. Celeste went, and a man named Diederichs asked for me, and immediately thereafter for you. Celeste pointed out that you were not there and that I was in bed. She came to ask whether I would see him, and when she went to fetch him heard mumbling and Major du Preez, Special Branch, appeared out of the passage darkness. I asked them their authority, they said C.I.D. Diederichs wanted to know where you were. I told them that I didn't know, that I hadn't seen you since the previous Monday. He asked whether you wouldn't telephone me and I said that you were probably too lazy for that. He suggested that I wasn't really sick, asked one or two more questions which must have been trivial, since I cannot remember them. I know that I completely failed to convince them. (I failed to convince myself that I did not know your whereabouts.) They left without Major du Preez saying a word.

Wolf is Jewish, and had lived in Hitler's Germany until the age of twelve. He knew the meaning of the midnight knock at the door. Almost immediately after this incident, he left South Africa. He knew that these arrests would not be the last. He had been politically active.

I spent nearly five months in Swaziland doing odd jobs and collecting my thoughts to write this book. I had not wanted to embarrass the local government or the people of the territory, and did nothing political. The laws of Swaziland require newcomers to apply for temporary residence if their stay is to exceed three months; I had to sign a declaration (which I did under protest) that I would not engage in any political activity, even though I had spontaneously given such an oral undertaking to the authorities. The relevant part of the declaration is given below:

It is a condition of this permit that you shall not take an active part in the politics of this territory or of either of the other High Commission territories *or of any territory bordering on any of the High Commission territories* [my italics].

For the purposes of this permit the words 'taking an active part in politics' include—

(i) writing for publication or causing to be printed or published in any manner any matter of a political nature;

(ii) making a speech relating to any such matter;

(iii) taking any part in the creation, direction, organization or activities of any political organization,

but do not include mere membership of a political party or the registering of a vote. This permit may be cancelled at any time without any reason being assigned therefor. If you fail to observe the condition mentioned above or any condition which may subsequently be notified to you, you will be guilty of an offence and liable to the penalties set out in section 21 of the proclamation.

In the early stages of the state of emergency, the Minister of Justice, Mr F. C. Erasmus, said that the emergency could not be lifted because a number of persons had escaped the net and 'were engaged in political activity against the security of the state'. He was, he said, negotiating with the British Government for their return. But the British Secretary of State for Commonwealth Relations soon made it clear that there was no question of returning anyone, and the Government did not dare to test its various charges against anyone by extradition. There were times during my stay in Swaziland when I was anxious to return to the Union, if necessary, to be with my colleagues in prison. But the Liberals advised me strongly against it. Feeling was high against me even in Swaziland; in the Union I would certainly not be safe.

On several occasions in Swaziland I missed assault by South Africans by a hair's breadth. There were also two or three attempts at abduction, not only of myself, but — much earlier — of Bishop Reeves.

The night of the attempt on Dr Verwoerd's life, I was to meet a friend in an hotel lounge. While I was waiting, I was joined by

a local resident who had previously been fairly friendly. An Afrikaner friend of his came past and stopped to talk. We were introduced. His first impulse, I could see, was to lash out, but he re-
strained himself, though his face became red with anger.

'You're Patrick van Rensburg,' he said. 'You're sure you're
Patrick van Rensburg?' He emphasized the 'Patrick' in his heavy
Afrikaans accent so that it became 'Petrick' with a rolled 'r'. I
was taken aback by the intensity of the man's reaction to meeting
me, and did not think it wise to make any jokes about my being
convinced that I was myself.

'You mean you're the man who went to England to organize
the boycott?' He went through my record. I had worked in the
diplomatic service and had resigned. Yes. Then I went to whip
up hatred against South Africa. He spoke in Afrikaans.

'Tell me,' he added, 'are you a Christian — or what?'

I said I was a Christian.

'You're not a Communist?'

'No, I am not.' There was a slight pause, and I thought perhaps he was allowing me to state my case, but he interrupted me.

'I used to be a Smuts man,' he said. 'But after today, I am behind the Government. If Dr Verwoerd dies, it will go hard with
people like you. We hold your sort responsible for this. If the
Government shoots people like you and every agitator among the
kaffirs, they will have my full support. Smuts would have known
how to deal with you people. He didn't hesitate to shoot down our
own people when he thought he had to.'

He nodded to his friend, who was a little shocked at such fury
and intensity, and then left. Later in the evening, after I had
gone home, he brought a party of five from a construction camp
near Mbabane to 'introduce' to me.

In early September I made my way from Swaziland to Bechuanaland, being helped to get there by friendly people. The Chairman of the Liberal Party, Peter Brown, had written to me, suggest-
ing that for some while, at least, I could do more useful work
outside than inside the Union, where my safety could never be

guaranteed and where I would probably be banned and politically hamstrung.

I met up by arrangement with a number of people at a point near Francistown in Bechuanaland. They were all people who had had, for various reasons, to leave the Union. After a few days of waiting, an aircraft from Ghana Airways landed at Francistown to collect us. We tried to attract as little attention as possible in Francistown, where we gathered on the morning of September 14th.

For weeks and months I had lived in a hostile atmosphere, and I felt a great sense of relief when I saw the plane touch down. But there were still a few tense moments ahead. We drove into the airport precincts in a hired lorry. The airfield belonged to the Native Recruiting Corporation; and six or seven of their White South African employers stood watching our arrival, their backs against the wall of the hangar, facing the plane.

I got off the lorry and walked towards the plane. The driver wanted to bring the lorry close up to the plane to unload baggage more quickly. I was three-quarters of the way to the aircraft when one of the employers of the Corporation, a huge, burly man, broke away from his group to prevent the lorry from approaching the plane. I turned round to see what was happening. The lorry had stopped and the burly man was gesticulating angrily at the African driver. Then he swung round, walking back to rejoin his group, and on his way he noticed that I was looking at him. He halted and looked at me, almost inquiringly. For the space of the next few seconds he waited hopefully for me to give just one sign of disapproval of what he had done. His behaviour towards the driver was uncouth, and now he looked nasty and menacing. I turned and climbed the steps of the aircraft. Not now. Not just as I was about to leave. Then we were gone; we were above it all. It was none too soon.

When we stopped down at Elisabethville, a patrol of soldiers surrounded the aircraft with fixed bayonets. There had been talk of Ghana's invading Katanga, and here was a Ghana Airways plane landing. After an hour of waiting, we were allowed off the plane, but were confined for the night to the airport restaurant, where we slept on the floor — with an armed guard of eight bayonets at the ready throughout the night.

We arrived in Accra two days later. I met Tennyson Makiwane again. He was one of the representatives in Accra of the South African United Front, which had been created some time earlier. For some reason he seemed almost to want to avoid meeting me, though we had worked well together in London. When we finally had an opportunity to talk, he told me that as a matter of principle the United Front had agreed that no organization with White members could join it. When the representatives of the African National Congress and the Pan-Africanist Congress (which had been — and still are — at loggerheads *in* the Union) had come abroad, they were told by the 'independent African states that they would not get anywhere unless they united'. They united after they had reached a compromise, 'which the P.A.C. had insisted on', to the effect that 'no Whites be allowed into the United Front'. The United Front represents three organizations in South Africa — the African National Congress, the Pan-Africanist Congress, the South African Indian Congress and two bodies in South West Africa.

The P.A.C. representative in Accra behaved towards me as if he had some old score to settle, although we had never met. He seized on every possible opportunity to try to embarrass, discomfort and humiliate me. The A.N.C. men who had come up with me from the Union were fiercely critical of this man, labelling him anti-White. We have since met again and are now better friends.

From the Ghanaians themselves, I had nothing but courtesy and helpfulness wherever I went. After spending three pleasant weeks in Accra marred only by the deliberate discourtesy of one man, I left for London.

When I look back on the development of my thinking over the last few years, I must admit that I have fallen into some of the pitfalls that I originally hoped to avoid. I did, to a certain extent, become something of a Negrophil, and the more I have had to do with Africans, the more I have been attracted by many of them as people. At the same time, however, I have never lost my basic sympathy for Afrikanerdom, and indeed, much of what I do constitutes an attempt to save the Afrikaners from themselves.

I had certainly been subjected to what I might call a brutalizing process. As the regime shows itself to be worse and worse, so one is ready to fight it with sharper weapons. Indeed, as so many avenues of opposition are closed to one by more and more laws, if resistance is to continue at all, it must be by means made unlawful. Boycott is hardly a traditional liberal instrument of opposition, but the excesses of racialist government become so extreme that temperamental and other objections to such things are soon overcome. Even one's political thinking is subjected to change. Liberalism cannot flourish in conditions of extreme racial hatred, embittered nationalism and widespread and crippling poverty. People deprived of their land, for instance, will demand a quicker redistribution of it than liberal methods alone can offer — and they will be entitled to it.

In retrospect, I must confess that I found it easier to *engage* in the more drastic opposition abroad than at home. The threat of punishment was less imminent and the freedom from immediate fear allowed a freer rein. It is only now that I have sat down to think about this that I have become conscious of it, and I feel that my conviction perhaps still needs a trial by ordeal in South Africa itself, sterner than I have yet experienced.

Racialism is obviously one of the vexed problems of Africa. It is also a very intricate one, and there are signs that it is becoming inverted. It is an inevitable consequence of White domination and prejudice that some Africans should react equally violently against Whites, and they see no reason then why they should discriminate between 'good' and 'bad' Whites. I have devoted a part of this book to a discussion of this question.

Here, too, there are pitfalls to be avoided. Too many people are inclined to call Africans anti-White just because they fight against racial domination and White privilege. These are the kind of people who also call liberalism 'appeasement'. I cannot see how it can be appeasement to advocate that people should have what they are entitled to, or to have returned to them that which has been unfairly taken away.

I will fight any form of racialism — when I am convinced that it *is* racialism. Anti-Whiteism is racialism, however understandable a reaction it may be, and much as I believe one should show understanding in dealing with it, one must show firmness also. I am deeply inspired when I find (as I do often) Africans themselves condemning it with vigour. It is possible that it may become a more widespread reaction; it may well be that when Africans have gained power throughout Africa, it will raise its ugly head in places. But because Africans will not fear the Whites as the Whites have feared them, it may soon die out. Certainly, fear has been one of the mainstays of White prejudice. For preference I should like to see racialism die out altogether when we smash it in South Africa in its present form. But when the boot is on the other foot can the Whites in South Africa reasonably hope for any better treatment than the Negroes will by then be getting in the American South? And can I or anyone else really complain about various manifestations of anti-Whiteism in Africa, when coloured and black men looking for accommodation or employment in Britain are refused simply because they are dark?

If humanity is to be indivisible, then the fight against racialism and prejudice should be so too, and I will be the ally of the Jew against anti-Semitism, of the American Negro in the Deep South, of the Jamaican racially insulted in Britain, of both Walloon and Fleming in their mutual antagonism in Belgium, of the Protestant in Spain and of the Catholic in Ulster, but above all — now — of my black, coloured and Indian compatriots, who are suffering from the effects of a racialism whose devastation of human dignity has probably been exceeded only once in recent times.

PART TWO

GUILTY LAND

CHAPTER I

THE GOD OF OUR FATHERS

I am now more than ever convinced
that the sins of this guilty land will
not be washed away but by blood.

JOHN BROWN, *on the eve of his
execution on December 2nd,* 1859

T HE last recorded words of John Brown are not quoted here
because I believe that the bloody events of the American
South must necessarily be repeated in South Africa, but because, by drawing attention to some of the parallels, I hope to give
a warning that may prevent organized mass bloodshed.

To provide a solution, we must know the problem. We have
also to examine the state of mind of the country's rulers, which in
turn means looking at the history of the country. Others have told
the story of South Africa more ably than I, and there have been
better analyses of the current political situation than the one I am
now producing, but while one analysis of a human problem may
be better than another, rarely is any single one complete. Because
I believe I understand the points of view of both Afrikaner and
African, and because I believe I am — partly because of that
understanding — objective, I may perhaps have some evidence to
add.

In dealing with the history I have left out dates because this
is not so much a chronological survey as an attempt to show
the development of influences that have led to present-day
attitudes.

The first White settlers came to the Cape shortly after Jan van
Riebeeck's arrival three hundred years ago. His mission was to

establish, in the Cape, a revictualling post for ships of the Dutch East India Company passing between Europe and the East. The settlers, it was hoped, would sell cattle, corn and wine to the Company.

Soon friction arose between the settlers and the Hottentots they found living in the Cape. Within two years, the settlers, who had no say in the local government, began to present lists of grievances to the Company. By this time, the first slaves were being imported from the Dutch East Indies, and the permanent White population of the settlement began to grow. Immigrants (including Huguenots) came in; many Company officials retired to live in the Cape; and the lovely peninsula attracted to its shores a few passengers from passing ships. A shortage of marriageable women led to some intermarriage between Europeans and freed Malay slaves and Hottentots.

As the White population increased, the colony spread farther inland. The settlers went in search of more land, or they left in exasperation at the imposed government of the Company. The trekking settlers developed a community of interests, as a result of their disputes with the Hottentots and their shared discontent with Company rule. Their common enemies and the hazards they faced together in wild and undiscovered country served to forge more strongly the bonds that were tying them together as 'a people'. It was also their movement inland that led, a century later, to the settlers' first contact with the Bantu tribes, a people quite different from and much darker than the Hottentots.

The settlers were essentially simple people, for they were predominantly of peasant stock and of little education. The trekking settlers further isolated themselves by venturing into a wilderness, forsaking even the comparative civilization of Cape Town, and carrying with them only their own limited concept of culture. In Europe they would not, of course, have had contact with the world of scholars; but in the Cape they soon lost contact with even their own level of thought in Europe, and those who trekked soon forsook the Cape peninsula. After 1652 they were, to all intents and purposes, cut off from the stream of world history, for in those days a sailing ship took between three and four months to sail from Europe to the Cape, only about thirty-five ships passed the Cape each year, and the Trekkers had removed themselves a further journey of several weeks inland.

The Company tried to extend the frontiers of its jurisdiction to keep pace with the dispersal of the people and to maintain authority over them — especially as regards collecting taxes — and their resistance to the Company united them still further.

But the strongest bond was their religion. The Bible was the cornerstone of all that they believed in. Some of them could do no more than 'half-read, half-recite' the Scriptures. There were certainly no learned theologians among them. They became accustomed to loneliness and isolation; indeed, isolation was the state of mind they knew best; and in such circumstances men often rely most heavily on their religious beliefs. Theirs was the Reformation of 1652, which they now proceeded to develop in their own way.

The Cape peninsula which they had left is remarkably beautiful. The climate resembles that of the Mediterranean and there is plenty of rain. The whole of the Eastern seaboard, too, is well watered, and some of the Trekkers moved there. But a little inland are the Little Karoo and the Great Karoo — vast stretches of arid land covered with thorn bushes, wide and open, with an occasional outcrop of rock. It is a bleak and desolate country; here the Trekkers settled.

It might have been the wilderness of Israel. Certainly these nomads, with their ox-wagons, their herds and flocks, their large families, their slaves and servants, quickly identified themselves with the patriarchs of the Old Testament. Their physical circumstances alone made the comparison a compelling one, especially since the Bible was virtually the only book they read. The Old Testament is the story of a chosen people. When the Trekkers met the Hottentots and Bushmen, men who differed from them in colour and culture and who were a 'heathen' people, their identification of themselves with the Israelites was perhaps inevitable.

Two religious influences shaped their attitudes towards the Hottentots and the Bushmen and, a century later, the Bantu. There was the precedent of the Old Testament and there was their own limited conception of Predestination. The Old Testament told them that the peoples they met were for ever inferior in the sight of God; their view of Predestination was to reinforce the idea that the inferiority was unchangeable. This was the core of the Christian message, as they saw it. In their contacts with the dark-skinned people — a people they met only as slaves and servants — this was the message they conveyed. The Bible was read every night in the Trekker family and the 'household' staff were permitted to listen to the reading. But, like the Israelites of old, the Trekkers did not proselytize.

The two differences between White and Black — of colour and of culture — were regarded as immutable and interrelated, and to individuals they further implied an inherent difference in intelligence, talent and general human ability.

The Trekkers' identification with the Israelites has been well described by one of South Africa's leading Afrikaans historians, Dr G. D. Scholtz, in a speech to the Nationalist-inclined South African Bureau of Racial Affairs. 'It was his religion which enabled the Afrikaner to remain in existence among the non-Whites, because it made him compare his own position with that of Israel — and as the duty had rested on Israel not to mingle with the surrounding heathens, so it also became the duty of the Afrikaner not to associate with the non-Whites. The eighteenth-century Afrikaner felt this even more strongly than the seventeenth-century Netherlander. His religion was even to lead him to look down on the non-Whites as completely beneath him.

'Thus it was that General J. W. Janssens wrote of the Afrikaners that "they describe themselves as *humans* and Christians, and the Kaffirs and Hottentots as heathens; and by believing in this they permit themselves everything. A brother of Thomas Ferreira is reputed to have certain literature and to have discovered that the Hottentots are the descendants of Ham and thus condemned by God to servitude and maltreatment." It was not only the brother of Thomas Ferreira who thought so — the great majority of Afrikaners probably cherished the same viewpoint. Even today it has not completely died out.'

Personally I believe that it is as prevalent today as it was then.

The people who stayed in and near Cape Town retained some link, however tenuous, with the outside world, and although many of them thought as the Trekkers did, there was not the same co-hesion, nor the same obsession.

But in the case of the Trekkers, their interpretation of the Bible determined their attitude towards the black man. Furthermore, their view of themselves as the Israelite patriarchs had a positive effect in giving them the inner bonds of unity that are necessary to the growth of nationhood.

It is easy to condemn these early settlers out of hand, and to forget that one is dealing with human beings. The Afrikaners are a generous, hospitable, courageous and kind people, cursed only with this one blind spot — one so tragic for themselves and others. But their reliance on the Bible, which produced this regrettable trait in them, also gave them many of the fine qualities taught by Judaeo-Christianity.

Who is to say that many others would not have reacted similarly in the same situation?

When the British occupied the Cape for the first time in the early nineteenth century, some hundred and fifty years after the arrival of the first settlers, the Trekkers already had some of the features of 'a people'.

Living so much in isolation, they naturally developed a new dialect of the language they spoke. They were cut off from the source of their original language, and there were many new in-fluences around them that tended to stimulate change. Difficulties of education and the lack of teachers led to a simplification of

Dutch. It became increasingly difficult for the parents of successive generations to correct mistakes, and the complicated grammatical structures of Dutch were broken down. Spelling was made easier, and though the first simplifications were made in the spoken language only, they were eventually reflected in the written. This development of a dialect was important in the growth of Afrikaner nationhood. The subsequent attempts of the British administration especially under Lord Charles Somerset, to suppress it in favour of English made the Afrikaners all the more determined to safeguard it.

But the most important development over the next centuries was the growing friction between the Trekkers and the native Africans. These clashes arose over land ownership and with them a kind of economic competition between the races was introduced.

The people on both sides were largely pastoral. They had grown accustomed to having large tracts of land on which their herds could graze. The Trekkers were always on the move in their search for land, and as some moved on, others remained to settle. On the death of a father, the younger sons pushed on, leaving the farm to the eldest rather than subdivide it, for families were invariably large.

The Trekkers clashed first with the Hottentots and the Bushmen, but neither was a formidable enemy, and neither ever settled on land even for a short space of time. But the Bantu, who began their migration southwards at about the time of the arrival of the first Whites in the Cape, were a much more settled people. Their migrations were slow-moving. A tribe would settle and a clan might then break off to move somewhere else and found a new dynasty. The Zulus settled in the far north-east, in what is now Natal. Their relatives, the Xhosas, migrated south-west in the direction of the advancing Boers.

South Africa's land surface is a little under half a million square miles. France, Germany, and Italy could be comfortably fitted into it. There were probably fewer than thirty thousand Boers and less than a million Africans in all this land when the two first met. Some of the settlers were already of the fourth generation in Africa, and we have seen how they would have had a ready-made attitude towards the Bantu. Most of the Boers were at this time spread out over the south-eastern Cape, itself a vast area. Various Bantu tribes were scattered about in what now constitutes the Transvaal, Natal and the eastern Orange Free State.

Neither Trekker nor Bantu had ever known any shortage of land. In their wanderings both had moved into vast uninhabited areas. Both sides regarded it as their right to settle in these empty lands, but the Bantu did not have the same concept of land owner-ship as the Boers. There was rarely any idea of personal tenure among the Bantu, and they neither understood nor conceded the Boer theory of owning land simply by virtue of possession. Indeed, even when Bantu chiefs signed a treaty with individual Boers or with Boer leaders, ceding land to them, they never regarded the land as having passed from them to the exclusive and permanent use and possession of the Boers. They intended to do no more than give the Boers the same rights over the land as individual tribes-men had. Of course, when the tribesmen came to exercise the rights they imagined they retained over the lands occupied by the Boers, the Boers, mistaking their motives, resisted the aggression and were in turn attacked by the tribesmen.

The Boers who had trekked across the arid Karoo found that it was neither technically nor agriculturally possible to develop pas-tures for fodder, as by then was the practice in a crowded Europe. In a little country like Holland, where land was short and nomadic pastoralism was part of prehistory, it was necessary to grow fodders that could give large yields from a small acreage. Here there were vast areas of grasslands, some greener than others, but always enough for all.

Both Boer and Bantu developed what might be called a 'ranch complex'. For each this became part of a way of life, a tradition that needed no argument or explanation to sustain it. Their farm-ing methods were extensive rather than intensive, and when they met, they did not change them. For example, when Boer and

Xhosa encountered each other in the eastern Cape, a fertile, well-watered area, each group had either to modify its ambitions and accept less land — or meet the opposition. The Trekkers could not go back because there were settlers on the land they had left behind them. The Xhosas, too, had left clans scattered sparsely about the country they had crossed who would fight to maintain their newly-acquired lands.

The Bantu who went to the Boer lands to exercise their traditional rights were repulsed. They attacked the Boers, who thereafter banded together for reprisals. Conquest of the land and the maintenance of their 'rights' by force became the only way in which the Boers could ensure personal tenure. When attacked, the Trekkers soon made it their practice to take as much cattle from the Bantu as they pleased, as a form of punishment. On their side, the Bantu naturally spread the word that wherever the Boers went, they would insist on exclusive use of the land and intended to conquer the Bantu to get it. The Boers, of course, viewed the Bantu disrespect of the treaties that had been signed as a sign of innate treachery. Neither side was able to understand the attitude of the other. Thus, during the first twenty years of the nineteenth century, three major battles, known as the Kaffir Wars, were fought.

The events of these years left their mark on the Boer mind. We have already seen the influence of religion. The Kaffir Wars taught the Trekkers the simple arithmetic of the situation which faced them, and demonstrated the numerical preponderance of the Africans. Here were masses of 'heathen savages', a people 'inferior in the sight of God', 'ordained by God's laws to a lower station in life'. In the eyes of the Boers, the Bantu were doing more than simply fighting over the land. They were challenging the laws of God; they were challenging a chosen people, and they were doing so as heathens against Christians, as forces of evil. They had to be subjugated so that the natural order of life could be restored. I believe it was in these circumstances that the Boers conceived the political theory that since the forces of darkness are ever seeking the overthrow of the forces of light, the African must be dominated lest he dominate. We shall encounter this belief again and again.

This did not mean that the Boers ever set out to exterminate the Africans. The African was ordained to servility in life, and not to release from bondage in death. The Trekkers' law was the law of Israel: 'Thou shalt not kill.' Only such killing as was necessary to put down the revolt of heathen forces, and in self-defence, was permissible.

The economy of the Boers, such as it was, was built on the labour of the Hottentots and the slaves, and later a few of the Xhosas. One hundred years after the first settlement of the Cape, there were 11,815 Whites and 12,398 slaves living there. In addition, there were Hottentots in the Boer service who were technically not slaves. A Dutch seaman, C. de Jong, writing of the state of mind of the settlers at the Cape, said: 'This too far-reaching pride results in laziness. Few Whites will put their hands to farm work, or use their arms in a store; that is slave work! What are the slaves for? is their answer.' Many other observers said the same thing.

During the course of these conflicts between Boer and Xhosa the British reoccupied the Cape. The new Administration was tinged with some of the liberal thinking then gaining ground in Britain. At the same time, a new kind of missionary began to arrive, preaching ideas of equality. We shall see, in the next chapter, how this contributed to the Great Trek. But one of the results of the changed administration was the abolition of slavery, which meant that the Boers had to turn elsewhere for their labour.

The Boers had always conveyed the Christian message as they saw it to their household staffs, who were permitted to hear readings from the Bible. Thus they had created a caste system in embryo, where both those dominated and those dominating accepted their respective positions as a matter of faith. But the Boers had not hitherto gone out to preach in a missionary sense. From the time of the arrival of these liberal missionaries, however, there was an increase in missionary endeavour on the part of the Boers, and the conclusion is inescapable that to the great majority of the

67

Trekkers the aim of this Christianization was to show the native African the futility of resisting against his predestined fate. There were, of course, individual deviations from this thinking, but it was the central tendency of Boer religious philosophy.

It was understandable that the Afrikaners should reject the teachings of universal love introduced by the British missionaries, notably the Rev. Dr John Philip, first because these teachings were utterly foreign to their whole understanding and belief, and secondly because they upset the traditional relationship that they had established with such Africans as were already in their service. We have seen that the economic class structure followed colour differences. This had the effect of strengthening the religious beliefs which sustained this position, and giving the Boers more practical reason to defend them.

The arrival of the missionaries coincided with the period when the Trekkers were finding the Africans most difficult, and in retrospect the two things have acquired a cause and effect relationship. Certainly, the missionaries and their new ideas could be blamed for the abolition of slavery.

To escape from British influence and its 'harmful' consequences and to go somewhere where they could establish their own states and rule the Africans in their own way, the Boers embarked on what is known as the Great Trek. Only by so doing could they be sure of their future. They had to dominate the African, harnessing as much of his labour as was necessary, but otherwise keeping him apart, and so ordering affairs that he was not rebellious against their authority and against the laws of God as they saw them. Philip suggested that the 'cheap labour' policy also influenced the Boer standpoint on African land and stock ownership, because so long as the Bantu had land and cattle enough to support them, labour would be in short supply.

The Trekkers split up into various parties under different leaders, and each party set out in a different direction. Piet Retief, one of the Trekker leaders, moved into the area now known as Natal where Dingane was the ruler of the powerful Zulus. Retief went to Dingane to sign a treaty with him in order to obtain a cession of land. The Trekkers had not yet learnt that this was meaningless to the Africans, but it is highly probable that stories about the Trekkers had preceded Retief. Dingane would have known the pattern of these treaties; he would have known that the Boer objective was to get exclusive use of the lands, an idea which was to him incomprehensible. A treaty was almost a declaration of war, because it always meant that as soon as it was signed, the Africans had to forfeit their lands. Dingane, playing for time, insisted as a condition of signing the treaty that Retief first recover cattle stolen from him by a neighbouring tribe. Retief did this and returned, which must have frightened Dingane even more, for it was an indication, by comparison with the neighbouring tribe, of Retief's military strength. Dingane had, in the past, murdered his half-brother Shaka, the founder of the Zulu nation. He was a perfidious man and a ruthless dictator, who was eventually overthrown by his own people. What followed was in keeping with his character.

Retief and his party were persuaded to leave their weapons outside the royal enclosure when they went in to sign the treaty. To have taken their weapons in, they were told, might have been construed as a sign of aggression. After the treaty was signed, Dingane suddenly shouted, 'Kill the Wizards,' and the whole party was brutally murdered. The Zulus immediately followed this up with the slaughter of a party of Trekkers who were at Weenen, awaiting the return of Retief. All were murdered, except one man who escaped to warn other Trekkers. To the Boers these killings were the final proof of the 'savagery' of the Bantu, and because of this they are one of the most important events in Afrikaner history.

Most of the Trekker parties were soon rounded up, and they banded together to avenge the murder of Retief. At the Battle of Blood River, where they met the Zulus, the Boers formed a *laager*, which is a circle of ox-wagons with thorn-bushes between them. Inside, they awaited the onslaught of the Zulus, who attacked in a half-moon column. The Boer women loaded the rifles of their men, who fired volley after volley into the Zulu ranks, which re-formed after each unsuccessful attack and charged again and again.

This battle, fought on December 16th, 1838, crushed the power of the Zulus, who had been the most powerful of all the Bantu tribes. Every year since, this day has been celebrated in South Africa as the 'Day of the Covenant', because the Voortrekkers had vowed that if God gave them victory that day, they would build a 'church of the vow' and celebrate the day of victory in per-petuity. The act of 'covenanting' with God is a further example of Trekker identification with the Israelites; the victory seemed to vindicate their theory. It seemed, furthermore, to prove that the Trekkers were a people chosen above the 'Black heathen savage', and to confirm their conception of the Bantu as inferior beings. More than anything else, the event served to weld even closer the inner bonds of Afrikaner unity. If the Boers had begun to believe, after the Kaffir Wars in the eastern Cape, that they had to dominate or be dominated, the murder of Retief and the slaughter at Weenen turned this into a powerful and obsessive conviction. Another belief was added: it was 'God led us through Blood River; He will do the same in another Blood River.'

CHAPTER II

A HOUSE DIVIDED

Ex unitate vires.
SOUTH AFRICA'S MOTTO

T H E first British occupation of the Cape was short. It was a strategic measure taken during the Napoleonic wars. Some twenty-five years later the British returned, this time with the intention of staying. It was colonization in earnest. The Boers, who had already been at the Cape for well over a hundred and fifty years, regarded themselves as a nation. Their attitude towards the indigenous peoples was already well defined, as was their view of the inept, indifferent and unrepresentative Government of the Cape by the Dutch East India Company. They also had what was virtually a new language of their own.

Soon after the British occupation, Lord Charles Somerset introduced his policy of making English the only official language, and the British brought within their jurisdiction the whole of the area that had been 'opened up' by the Boers. This extended the Cape Colony north of Cape Town into the Karoo, and eastwards for over five hundred miles.

The London Missionary Society soon took an active interest in the Cape. Not only their missionaries, but others, came to the new British colony. These people represented the liberal, humanistic spirit which was sweeping Europe. One of the most forceful exponents of the new ideas was Philip of the London Missionary Society. Such men bitterly opposed the existence of slavery, and they soon discovered and denounced the Boer view of the aboriginal people. Philip, helped in Britain by Wilberforce, tried to persuade the British Government to institute reforms in the

Cape. This made him and his fellow missionaries an object of hatred to the Boers. For a missionary to teach that 'all are one in Christ' was contrary to the understanding of a people nurtured in isolation on the Old Testament. Indeed, the hatred they have today for men like Michael Scott and Father Huddleston reflects the feelings they had for Philip a hundred and thirty years ago. Ten years after the British reoccupied the Cape, slavery was abolished. Some years earlier Philip had travelled to Britain to plead for this. Whether or not his voice had any effect, he carried most of the blame in Boer eyes. Hence the detestation today of travels to Britain by missionaries and others to appeal for aid.

The Boers felt intuitively that the spread of liberal ideas would not end with the abolition of slavery. They anticipated that the British Government would attempt to place the indigenous people, the Coloureds, and even the freed slaves, 'on an equal footing with the Christians'. Resentment of British colour policy was the principal reason for the Great Trek. All else the Boers might have forgiven. But in this, British policy was unacceptable. It was not only a calculated insult, but was also suspected of showing British determination to bring about the Boer downfall by swamping them with non-Whites. The British seemed to be prepared to place the Boer under the control of 'heathens', the 'forces of darkness'. The numerical superiority of the 'heathens' would ensure this if they were allowed to be equal to the Boers and the British. This, then, was the background to the Great Trek.

The Great Trek ushered in a new era in which race policies in South Africa were clearly divided. In the South, more particularly in the Cape, the policies introduced by the British led, when elections for representative government came, to the extension of the franchise to the Coloured and African people. In the north, the Boer policies meant in essence 'dominate or be dominated'. The policies of the present Government follow those of the Boers.

When the Trekkers left the Cape on their journey north, they felt quite sure that they were rid of the British for ever. Retief wrote at the time: 'We quit this colony under the full assurance that the English Government ... will allow us to govern ourselves without its interference.' Yet *four* years after the Battle of Blood River, and *three* years after the Republic of Natal had been founded, the British annexed Natal after a short struggle. Some years previously they had established Port Natal, later Durban. Natal came under the authority of the Governor of the Cape, who was prepared to discuss with the Trekkers the granting to them of a degree of independence. But he imposed conditions which were clearly unacceptable. These were that there should be no colour bar, no slavery, and no taking-over of native land. Most of the Trekkers left Natal in protest, moving into parts of what are now the Orange Free State and Transvaal. The British Government annexed much of the territory into which the Boers moved. They argued that since their occupation of the Cape, the Boers had become British subjects who could not simply abandon the obligations of citizenship. Wherever they went, they went as British subjects. They did not, by going, forfeit that citizenship. The territory they occupied became British territory, since it was settled by British subjects.

To the Boers, the British purpose seemed to be to impose on them the Cape colour policy and to subject them to Black domination. Their worst fears were confirmed when the franchise was extended 'without distinction of class or colour' in the elections for representative government in the Cape.

Three years after this, the Trekkers founded the Transvaal Republic. An uncertain and uneasy independence was maintained for about twenty years, until, after the discovery of diamonds in the Kimberley area, which had been annexed by the Transvaal Republic, the British annexed the Transvaal also. This was a new source of conflict. Two years after the annexation of their Republic the Boers rebelled, but were defeated and forced to accept proposals for a state under British suzerainty in the Transvaal.

Then gold was discovered on the Witwatersrand in the Transvaal, and attracted a huge influx of fortune-seekers. Rhodes became Prime Minister of the Cape and preached an immense British federation, which would include territory he had acquired north of the Transvaal, now Rhodesia. Kruger, President of the Transvaal Republic, denied the vote to the 'gold diggers', whom he called *Uitlanders,* or foreigners. If given the vote, he argued, they would swamp the Boers and turn them out of power. Because of the liberal British outlook on colour, this would open the way to eventual Black domination.

British imperialism was now entering its most indefensible phase. Rhodes and Sir Alfred Milner were its dominating agents. The discovery of gold meant that only the flimsiest of pretexts was necessary for British intervention in the Transvaal. Kruger, the massive guardian of the Boer tradition, appeared to give way under *Uitlander* pressure, but his concession was hardly worth the paper it was written on. The franchise would be granted but only after *fourteen years'* residence.

The ill-starred Jameson Raid, led by Dr Starr Jameson, from Rhodesia, was intended to spark off a revolt among the *Uitlanders* but failed. Still, all the ingredients of war were there, and at the turn of the century it came. Again, one of the reasons given for the war was the Afrikaner attitude towards the Africans. The British Government of the day was very different from its mid-nineteenth-century predecessor; its protestations of liberalism were clearly only a pretext for imperialism. Kruger and the Boers provided reason enough for war, but the British Government, persuaded by Rhodes and Milner, would probably have fought merely for the gold of the Transvaal.

The war lasted for two years. When it was over, there were two hundred thousand Afrikaners in concentration camps. Some four thousand women and sixteen thousand children died as a result of unhygienic conditions in the camps. Thousands upon thousands of acres of farm land were burnt by the British. Some ten thousand persons were, it is believed, displaced by the war.

In the Cape, many Afrikaners joined the Boers. As British subjects, they were executed for treason if captured.

The Liberals who came to power in Britain soon after the war set out to atone for it. They had opposed it strongly and bitterly. Emily Hobhouse, who went to South Africa to work in and protest about the concentration camps, was representative of a widespread feeling in England.

The war diverted British and world sympathy from the African people, to whom the Boers had consistently denied rights. A reaction set in to the fighting and the cruelties (accidental and calculated). There was a flood of sentimental sympathy for the Boers, and revulsion against the Tories. The work of Philip and the Boer domination of the Africans were forgotten in the general tide of disgust at the military excesses. And forgotten by the Liberals, of all people. They were magnanimous towards the defeated Afrikaners, and hoped that generous action might evoke a generous response. They were encouraged in their hopes and plans by the conciliatory spirit of Botha and Smuts, two of the outstanding Boer generals. Indeed, an accommodation seemed possible between the Afrikaners and the British settlers, who had, by and large, taken Britain's side. It also seemed possible that relations between the Boers and the British people and Government might improve. It was hoped that once such an accommodation was brought about — once the Afrikaners were convinced of British good will and sincerity under a Liberal government and saw that it was not Britain's intention to swamp the Boer vote — then of their own accord they might look differently on the Africans. A few voices in the Cape defended the rights of Africans and Coloureds when the National Convention met in Durban to discuss the settlement of Union. The Northerners at the Convention, predominantly Boer, fought tooth and nail against the inclusion in the settlement of voting rights for coloured people. But they were prevailed upon, for the sake of unity, to let the Africans and Coloureds of the Cape retain their existing rights. They even agreed to the entrenchment of these rights in the Cape. To alter them would need a two-thirds majority of the Union Senate and House of Assembly sitting together.

The Boer fight against the rights of coloured people should perhaps have been a warning. Instead, their concession over the Cape was taken as a good augury. When the settlement, as agreed by all the relevant parties in the Union, went to the House of Commons, some twenty-eight Labour members, twenty-six Liberals and three Irish Nationalists opposed it, though it obtained a majority of 157 votes. The opponents of the Act of Union gave very clear warnings of the dangers of its colour-bar provisions. One Labour member warned that they would force non-whites to adopt unconstitutional methods of opposition, and forecast the revival of Krugerism.

On May 31st, 1910, the Union was born. But soon the enthusiasm and excitement began to wear away and essential differences beneath the surface were revealed. The gamble taken by British Liberalism failed. The generous action did not evoke a generous response after the first years of Union. It failed, in my view, because the British did not come to grips with Afrikaner nationalism and had no proper understanding of it. It also failed because of subsequent unforeseeable events. There are, as I hope to show, lessons that liberalism everywhere should have learnt from this; it is important that the liberals of South Africa, at least, should learn them. There might be a parallel ahead.

At the first elections after Union the state of the parties in Parliament was as follows:

South African Party (Botha, Smuts and Hertzog)   66 seats

Unionists (Pro-British : Dr Starr Jameson)   39 ,,
Natal Independents (Pro-British)   11 ,,
Labour Party   4 ,,

Most Afrikaners supported Botha and Smuts. Many of the English-speaking people of the Cape and most of its qualified

African and Coloured voters, besides most of the former Transvaal *Uitlanders,* voted for Dr Jameson's Unionists.

Between December 1911 and December 1912, Hertzog — one of the three Boer generals who led the Afrikaners — made four speeches which raised a storm throughout the country. He spoke of two streams of life in South Africa, which included the old Dutch-speaking and the old English-speaking sections, both of whom had no other country. But there was a third class, he said, which, though South Africans from a legal point of view, had always a strong feeling for their motherland and wished to return to it. The national spirit, he said, must be Dutch and English, but at the elections this third class of people had used the cry of 'Vote British', and it was this spirit that kept the English-speaking people away from the Dutch. He came back to the theme in his other speeches, and in one questioned whether the Dutch language was getting equal treatment with English, the other official language. He said that the South African should be *baas* (boss). He would not allow himself to be governed by foreign fortune-seekers. Hertzog's attacks were directed against the Unionists, and particularly Dr Jameson. He was accused of racialism, and political commentators concluded that it was his view that conciliation did not mean the abandonment of the ideal of an Afrikaner nation. He was said to be advocating a two-stream policy, which meant the development of two separate groups co-operating closely.

In response to the pressure, the Prime Minister, Louis Botha, asked Hertzog to resign. Hertzog refused, and Botha was obliged to resign himself and reconstitute his cabinet, leaving Hertzog out.

In January 1914, Hertzog formed the National Party. Its declared native policy was that 'in our attitude towards the Natives, the fundamental principle is the supremacy of the European population in a spirit of Christian trusteeship, utterly rejecting every attempt to mix the races.' The Party's policy towards the two White language groups was one of 'South Africa first'.

Later in the same year, Britain went to war with Germany. It was a crucial test of the unity of Boer and Briton. Only twelve years previously, the two had been fighting each other in a war which had left bitter memories. Botha and Smuts appeared to be willing to join Britain against Germany because they accepted South Africa as part of the Empire, and because they felt that to do so was a logical extension of the new understanding with the English-speaking people. About the loyalties of the English there could be no more doubt than about the loyalties of Canadians, Australians or New Zealanders of British descent.

The Afrikaner had a different criterion. Was this war one which his own interests demanded he should enter? Were South African interests — as conceived and interpreted by the Afrikaner — imperilled by Germany? Should the Afrikaner be dragged into a war just because the English section felt it should be a belligerent party? Did not conciliation demand from the English some understanding of the Afrikaner point of view? Germany had, after all, befriended the Boers during the Boer War twelve years earlier.

Hertzog's newly-formed National Party condemned participation in the war, and in the Transvaal there was danger of an uprising under one of the former Boer generals, de la Rey. A man named Maritz who was in charge of the Union forces at Upington negotiated with the Germans in near-by South-West Africa in the hope of support for Afrikaner independence. This led to a full-scale rebellion, which spread southwards into the Cape from South-West Africa and was supported by many Afrikaners. One of the rebels, Jopie Fourie, was captured and executed — to become yet another Afrikaner martyr. The rebels were still hankering after their lost republics, and still wanting to avenge their defeat. The rebellion disinterred the bitter memories of the Boer War, and it showed that the World War had come too soon after Union to test the unity that had been attempted.

During the ten years after the start of the World War, Hertzog's Nationalists steadily increased their power in the Assembly. In 1915, soon after being joined by Dr D. F. Malan and his Cape

Afrikaner Party, his National Party won twenty-seven of the hundred and twenty seats in the House of Assembly. At the end of the war, the Afrikaner Nationalists even sent a delegation to the Peace Conference at Versailles to seek independence for South Africa, or for the former Boer republics. In 1920, the National Party won forty-four seats in the Assembly, and Smuts's South African Party only forty-one. By this time Botha was dead, and Smuts, his successor, had to form a coalition with the Unionists and independents. In the same year, the South African Party and the Unionists merged, Smuts called a snap election, and the enlarged South African Party won seventy-nine seats. The National Party moved forward one seat to forty-five. By 1924, it held sixty-three seats, Smuts was down to fifty-three, the Labour Party had eighteen, and the National and Labour Parties were able to form a coalition, the 'Pact Government'.

For the thirty-five years following the discovery of gold the conflict between White and White, between Britain and the Boer republics, was in the foreground. It seemed as if it had eclipsed the conflict between White and Black. But that conflict remained a very real one. With the selection of Louis Botha as Prime Minister of the Union, a deliberate choice had been made between the colour policies of the Cape and the North. The contest was between John X. Merriman, who until Union was Prime Minister of the Cape, and Louis Botha, who between the Boer War and 1910 was Premier of the Transvaal. The choice was a part of the mood of conciliation, and Mr Merriman, reflecting on it two months after Union, said rather wistfully, 'I wished most earnestly and desired to start Union upon Cape colonial lines rather than upon Transvaal lines. I thought the Cape Colony lines were safer.' He left no doubt at the end of his speech that one of the matters he was referring to was 'colour policy'.

Louis Botha was a Boer, but one deeply committed to the spirit of conciliation which had brought about Union, and who personified its spirit in his behaviour. Union had meant not only a compromise between the interests and viewpoints of English and

79

Afrikaner on matters quite apart from the 'native question', but on that matter too it had bridged the differing traditions of north and south. To Botha it was probably unthinkable to tamper with the entrenched voting rights of the Cape Coloureds and Africans. He opposed the retention of these rights at Union, but they were now a part of the bargain. For the future, he would press his own Boer view on the 'native question', but without fanaticism, and always in a spirit of compromise. The view of the English in the north was, in some respects, close to that of the Boers, and this strengthened Botha's hand against the Cape.

Botha may well have gone too far towards meeting the English in two other important matters. The first was the dismissal of Hertzog after his 'two stream' speech, and the second South Africa's participation in the war. But Botha's actions were part of the compromise that he judged to be correct.

Botha and Smuts had a powerful hold over the Boers. The two men had been outstanding generals; their prestige stood high among their people. If Union was a success, much of the credit for the success was theirs. It was largely their influence which held the Boers together in giving effect to the spirit of union in the years following 1910. When Botha died, Smuts kept up the tradition, and he too may have leaned too far towards the English in 1920, when he had to choose between the Unionists and the Nationalists for his coalition. He merged his own South African Party and the Unionists, who to Hertzog represented 'un-South Africa'. Certainly today, ten years after the death of Smuts, his prestige stands much higher in Britain and among the English of South Africa than it does among the Afrikaners.

The real, underlying conflict of the first fifteen years of Union was the fight between two ideologies for the allegiance of the Afrikaners, who predominated in an overwhelmingly White electorate. Botha and Smuts tried to convert Afrikaner opinion to the spirit of compromise and the policy of co-operation. Hertzog was set on a course that was to bring Afrikanerdom back to the spirit of the Great Trek and the Boer republics. It is possible that he did not then see the full implications of his course; for he was in fact taking a party of Boers on a trek — not a physical trek, but one no less real for that.

When he struck out, it was away from the *Uitlanders* who had brought such turmoil to the Transvaal, away from the Unionists and the more liberal 'colour' policies of the Cape, and towards Boer ideals. He may genuinely have hoped to take a large section of the English with him, but it was a vain hope. Few of the *Uitlanders* or the Cape English would set out along a road that must inevitably end in Boer republicanism.

There is no question but that events played into Hertzog's hands. The first World War was a terrible set-back to the spirit of unity. The extreme jingoistic, pro-British attitude of the Unionists seemed to the Boers intransigent, when compared with the conciliatory attitude of Botha. But one thing more than any other helped Hertzog. His kind of thinking about the *Africans* was that of the old Boers, whereas Botha was handicapped by his need and attempts to compromise with the Cape. Urbanization and industrialization brought in their wake the problem of economic competition between White and Black in the cities, and Hertzog's policies were of necessity more attractive to the Whites.

OH! TO BE IN ENGLAND

TH E attitudes of the English-speaking section of the South
African population developed quite differently from those
of the Boers. There were similarities, of course, but the differences were far more important.

The first British settlers came in 1820, fifteen years before the
Great Trek, clinging mainly to the eastern Cape coast, where they
landed, not far from the Boers and the Xhosas inland. They
founded a town, now Port Elizabeth, at Algoa Bay, and farther
east founded East London.

They came from a Europe very different from the Europe that
the first Dutch settlers had left. The humanistic and liberal influences acting on the Continent were perhaps strongest in Britain.
Not that most of the settlers were eminent humanists and liberals;
but their outlook was still quite different from that of the Boers
they encountered. Because during their first few years in the
eastern Cape, they experienced far fewer of the frustrations that
the Boers suffered under the new British occupation, and saw
only a little of the conflict with the Xhosas, it is extremely doubt-
ful whether they ever had a real understanding of the psychology
of the Afrikaners.

They may have had misgivings about the missionary work of
Philip, but they did not regard his work as contrary to morality or
against the laws of God. It was their own kind of religion which
Philip was preaching, and though they may have doubted its wis-
dom politically, they would never have argued against Philip on
religious grounds.

During the next two decades many English people came, especially to Natal. The English colonies were settled ones, the

newcomers having little of the wanderlust of the Trekkers. They came from Britain, where they had been accustomed to living huddled together, and indeed, when they arrived there were no longer the vast empty spaces that the Boers had found. The English did not have quite the same lust for land that the other groups had acquired. They were satisfied with what they found where they landed, and they established towns and villages, which the early Afrikaners had rarely done.

Once settled, these English colonists maintained their links with Europe and civilization. Shipping had progressed since the time of van Riebeeck; there were plenty of new settlers and there was regular correspondence with home. When the English clashed with the native Africans, they found them different — wild and un-developed — and they disliked them; but they did not think of them as immutably and permanently inferior.

The British Government's extension of the franchise to all races in the Cape, with restrictions and qualifications that applied to all races equally, made it electorally unprofitable for politicians to preach racial animosity. Over the years that the Cape Colony existed, this affected Boer and Briton alike, so that even among the Afrikaners of the Cape some kind of liberal approach existed in public, if not in private.

The British settlers of the Cape were an urban rather than a rural people, and their interests, their lives, their livelihoods, were centred round the towns. They put their roots down in the Cape as a part of Southern Africa and as a part of something other than Britain. They retained, nevertheless, strong sympathy with Britain, and for most of them there was pride in being British. In the conflicts they had with the Xhosas, they had the administra-tion on their side, and they were on the side of the administration. When the Anglo-Boer War broke out, they were on the British side, and many of the British soldiers came from among them.

The English settlers who came to Natal had similar experiences, but they had much less contact with Boers. Most of them arrived after the Battle of Blood River, after the Boer republic of Natal had been declared and subjected to British supervision, and after most of the Boers had trekked away in protest. By this time, too, the power of the Zulus was eclipsed, so that there remained only a certain measure of conflict with Dingane's people. The great majority of Zulus were settled within the tribal area of Zululand, essentially a part of the Zulu tribal empire and system. Meetings between Zulus and settlers were infrequent, a series of individual brushes. With the Boers gone and their method of administering the African gone with them, there was no focal point for a strong liberal reaction. Natal was, until 1893, ruled from the Cape, with a lieutenant-governor, locally resident, in charge. The franchise was opened to all races, as in the Cape, but it was more strongly qualified, and the Zulus, who lived apart from the colony, were not part of the electorate.

Many more Englishmen became farmers in Natal than in the Cape, but there too most of the immigrants settled in towns. The farmers used Black labour, but the Zulu's traditions were against work of this kind, so they were branded by the White farmers as lazy.

Sugar farming was the most profitable occupation in Natal, and as labour had to be found, it was brought from India. The first labourers came in 1860 as indentured workers. It was intended that they should return to India. Most were re-indentured again and again, and eventually they became a settled part of the population. They seemed unassimilable; they were called 'coolies' and in India many of them might have been *harijans* (untouchables). The local English were not prepared to absorb them and they retained, by and large, their religion, language and customs. Though they were labelled 'unassimilable', they became an integral part of the sugar economy of Natal. Some of them even came to own their own sugar farms. They worked hard, they saved, and they lived — as the Natal White has it — on the 'smell of an oil-rag'. They chewed betel-nut, ate curry, and their women wore saris. A few of them prospered and became better off than some of the Whites. The first arrivals were mainly Hindus; others, including Moslems, followed, and became traders, some of whom did well. Whites therefore soon regarded them as an economic threat, and racial prejudice grew up against them. The settlers also had prejudices against the Africans and these became stronger over the years. All in all Cape Liberalism did not take very strongly in Natal.

The English came to the Transvaal in very different circumstances. The first arrivals were diamond-hunters. In the great gold rush, Englishmen were part of a motley crew who came to the Witwatersrand. They were fortune-seekers, who differed in character from the settlers of Natal and the Cape. They came into the illiberal, strongly republican Boer sphere of influence, and for them the African's rights were hardly a pressing consideration. They were, as they were involved in politics, more concerned with their own treatment under the Kruger regime. As the years passed and they realized they had come to stay, the question of who should control the wealth of the Transvaal became important. The choice was between Kruger and Britain. Any choice, from their point of view, was better than Kruger, and as most of them were British anyway, they were in favour of war against Kruger.

There were, then, three kinds of English settler in South Africa. They came together in the war against the Boers, and the great majority of them were inclined to regard themselves as British. After Union, some of them strongly supported the spirit of conciliation. Many of those who did were from the Cape and John X. Merriman was perhaps their most outstanding spokesman. Many of them were members of Jameson's Unionist party, very pro-British and supporters of empire, whereas Natal was more independent-minded. (It had been a little sceptical about Union and was the only province in which the issue had to be put to a referendum; the majority for Union was small.)

After Union, many of the English were alienated by what they called Hertzog's racialism. They failed to understand the Boer reluctance to join the first world war, and they watched the subsequent growth of 'Hertzogism' with dismay. Over the years, in reaction to the rise of Afrikaner nationalism, many of them appeared to become more pro-British than ever, and were accused by the Afrikaners of having 'one foot in England'. Most of all, the Afrikaners resented very much the fact that few of them made any attempt to learn Afrikaans.

Industrialization and urbanization brought some of these people into conflict with Afrikaners and Africans, all seeking work. Because they were not attracted to Hertzog's programme, as the Afrikaner workers were, these drifted towards the all-White Labour Party.

In many respects English-speaking attitudes towards the African and other racial groups resemble those of the Afrikaner. There are, however, differences — most marked among people in the Cape. There is no longer any widespread liberalism even there, but what is true is that there are more English-speaking South Africans than Afrikaners who are liberals. What is also true is that, because their prejudices are less anchored to philosophic and religious doctrines than those of the Afrikaners, they are more amenable to pressures and more likely to make concessions when the pressures are great enough.

CHAPTER IV

DOMINATE OR BE DOMINATED

IN 1924, it seemed that Hertzog's ideology had won. But the battle was not yet over. Hertzog stood for pure Afrikaner nationalism; Smuts for the spirit of Union, for conciliation. Thousands of Afrikaners voted for Smuts and against Hertzog, whose National Party won sixty-three seats that year against Smuts's fifty-three. This left Colonel Cresswell's Labour Party with eighteen seats, holding the balance of power, and the Colonel allied his party with the Nationalists.

But already in 1922, the conflict between White and Black over jobs in urban areas had reached a crisis. There was violence and nearly a rebellion. Hertzog's victory at this point was not a victory for Afrikaner nationalism; for he came into power in coalition with a party that represented English-speaking workers as well as Afrikaners, and this was far from the final goal of the Afrikaner nationalists, who wanted to unite all Afrikaners and then to assimilate the English.

By 1929 Hertzog was nearer this goal. His National Party won seventy-eight seats, Smuts sixty-one, and Labour only eight. In 1933 the picture was more or less the same, but the world was in the throes of the great depression. When Britain went off the gold standard, Hertzog, wanting to show the country's independence, refused to follow suit. The Imperial Conference of 1930 had agreed to give legislative effect to the Balfour Declaration of 1926, which recognized the independence of the dominions. Hertzog, however, found it necessary to satisfy supporters like Dr Malan who felt that real independence presupposed republican status, but he was not yet independent of the kind of English support that the Labour Party gave him.

GUILTY LAND

The refusal to leave the gold standard precipitated a flight of capital, and the depression in South Africa was aggravated. In this time of crisis the country needed a national government that could subordinate the 'racial' issues, so Hertzog formed a coalition with Smuts, writing in his diary that if he had refused the pressure for coalition and Smuts's invitation, 'it would be said that we had refused the hand of friendship, and Smuts could not be blamed if he now made common cause with the Natal Devolutionists and Federationalists, thus giving the Afrikaans language and Afrikanerdom an irremediable blow.' But Malan and his followers, however, stood aloof from the coalition, believing that it was in itself a great blow to Afrikanerdom. In 1938, two years after Smuts and Hertzog had merged their parties, they won one hundred and eleven seats in the House of Assembly, while Dr Malan's National Party won twenty-seven.

Then came the Second World War, and the cabinet split. Hertzog was for benevolent neutrality; Smuts for joining Britain. Smuts won the division by thirteen votes, and reconstituted his Government in co-operation with the Natal Devolutionists and Federationalists.

Now a new struggle for the loyalties of the Afrikaner majority in the electorate opened between Hertzog and Dr Malan. Hertzog wanted to establish the fullest national independence; he wanted to raise the Afrikaner nation to a status of complete equality with the English; he wanted the Afrikaner to develop to the full his talents and potentialities; and he wanted the Boer native policy. In most of that he succeeded. South Africa became a completely independent and sovereign state. In 1936 Smuts had paid the price of coalition: the removal of the Africans in the Cape from the common voters' roll and their replacement on a separate roll.

But Malan believed that there was still a long way to travel along the path to the Afrikaner past. When in 1939 Hertzog voted with the Malan Nationalists against 'fighting Britain's war' there was hope of an Afrikaner reunification, but Hertzog was uneasy

88

DOMINATE OR BE DOMINATED

about Malan's policies. His own creation was becoming ugly and repulsive to him. Hertzog therefore resigned to form the Afrikaner Party, and finally, in the early days of the war, retired altogether.

Malan and his Nationalists, on the other hand, plunged head-long into militant Afrikaner nationalism, bitterly opposing the war. On January 17th, 1942, Dr Malan said in Parliament, as Leader of the Opposition, that the 'extension of the war did not come from Germany ... it was not due to Germany's urge to dominate the world ... but ... simply due to the scramble for allies on England's side. Our great duty is to face the danger that Germany may win, and we shall have then to consider what will be the best thing for South Africa, and the attitude of us on this side of the House is one which South Africa will yet be grateful for ... even though we are at war we want to withdraw from that war ... we wanted to preserve peace with Germany.'

Mr C. R. Swart, one of Dr Malan's chief lieutenants, now State President, had said a few months earlier that 'the signs, so far as we can judge, are that Germany has definitely won the war. The Nationalist Party is the only party that will be in a position to treat with the victor.'

In the wartime elections, Smuts's Party of Fusion won eighty-nine seats and Malan's National Party minority increased its representation from twenty-seven to forty-three. This showed that many Afrikaners were committed to the war; and indeed many of the Union's fighting soldiers were Afrikaners. Nevertheless, Malan had shown his ability to capture a large part of Hertzog's following with his extreme brand of Afrikaner nationalism.

After three years of peace, at the general elections of 1948, Malan won seventy seats and Smuts's United Party sixty-five. Smuts was defeated in his own constituency. The end of Malan's trek was in sight.

* * *

During the early days of Union, when Hertzog and Botha

89

joined battle for the loyalty of the Afrikaners, Hertzog had had the advantage. The Act of Union provided for a 'loading' of urban seats and an 'unloading' of rural seats. This meant — and still means — that the number of voters needed to send a member to Parliament could be nearly a third fewer in a rural than in an urban area. The 'quota' of electors for each constituency is determined by dividing the total number of registered voters in the country by the number of seats in the Assembly. But the number of electors in a rural constituency can be fifteen per cent less than the national quota, while the number for constituencies in the towns and cities can be fifteen per cent more. This can mean a total 'loading' of thirty per cent in favour of rural constituencies, which favours the Afrikaners because the rural areas have always been predominantly Afrikaans, and the Afrikaner way of life has always been essentially a rural tradition.

Botha had been obliged to compromise between his views and those of the Cape. On colour policy, this meant that he could not go the whole way with Hertzog, who was restricted by no concern to consider any views other than illiberal ones. At the same time, Botha knew that the English in the Transvaal and the Cape did not all take the 'Cape view', and this offset some of his disadvantage. In 1913 the Botha Government, at Hertzog's prompting, introduced the Natives Land Act, which defined the various tribal areas existing at the time. These were the pockets of land into which the Africans had been herded during their conflicts with the white man — the ever-decreasing heartlands of the various tribes, or the 'locations' that had been set aside for tribes under the Transvaal Republic, as the European occupation increased. Once the Act became law, Africans could not buy land outside areas defined as theirs.

There was also another way of appeasing the Afrikaner farmer. Pass laws, which had existed in the various colonies and republics since before Union, restricting the movement of Africans from place to place, were now used to reduce the number of Africans going to the cities and to maintain a good supply of Black labour in White farming areas.

But the greatest problem that faced the newly-born Union was the position of the 'poor Whites'. Here was another fertile source of Afrikaner voting-power. There were many poor Whites. Most were Afrikaners who were impoverished for a number of reasons. Some Whites were poor precisely because they regarded themselves as superior: they were not prepared to earn money by undertaking menial tasks and manual labour. Other 'poor Whites' or 'White kaffirs' — as they were frequently called in my own youth by those around me — were a hard core of people who were poor because they lacked the innate ability to better themselves. The tough life of the Trekkers in the wilderness had brought out fine qualities in many of them, but it was a life that challenged not so much intellectual prowess as physical endurance. Furthermore, the traditional attitude towards the land with its 'ranch-complex', having survived into an era of greater competition, pushed the inefficient to the bottom. Farming is not always easy in South Africa, with its extremes of drought and flood.

Once the Africans were confined to the minimum proportion of the land, it was no longer possible to make way for more Whites by driving the 'Kaffirs' out. By 1923, it is reliably estimated, there were a hundred and sixty thousand poor Whites — one-tenth of the White population. By this time, most of them were urbanized, driven by their poverty off the land and into the cities. But poor Whites who were unwilling to do 'kaffir work' on the farms were no more enthusiastic about it in the towns. One of the incidental results of Afrikaner urbanization was the development of an inferiority complex, especially in relation to the English. Although it was the Afrikaners who first penetrated the interior and opened up the country, although the agricultural economy depended on them, the real wealth of the country was in the hands of the British and the Jews, who together developed the gold mines and industry. When the poor country folk came wide-eyed to the towns, they were amazed by the achievements of more dynamic people and interpreted the wealth they found about them as a sign of the superiority of those who controlled these cities.

Hertzog preached his Afrikaner nationalism to the poor Whites. He hoped to encourage self-assertion among the Afrikaners; to give them pride in themselves, and to teach them to accept the dignity of labour. The key to their advance as a people lay in the possession of greater material wealth. That would also be a demonstration of their superiority over the African. 'Upliftment' of the poor White became the main task of Afrikaner nationalism. When Hertzog came to power in 1924, he had set out immediately to improve their lot. By 1926 the notorious 'Colour Bar' Act was in force, reserving certain jobs in mines for Whites. Between 1921 and 1928 the number of white unskilled railway labourers rose from 4,706 to 15,878. To provide jobs for poor Whites, Hertzog used the force of law on the mines and industry; he took them into the public service and on to the railways; he even established a steel industry, absorbing many of them in employment.

It was at this point that, in 1948, Malan took up the torch of Afrikaner nationalism. Dr Malan's rise to power was due to a certain amount of good fortune. His party was the main opposition to the Smuts wartime Government, which ruled for the first three post-war years and lost a certain amount of popularity in the process. But if any of the voters who chose Malan in pique at Smuts discovered their error, they did so too late, for as Dr Malan's programme unfolded, it became increasingly obvious that its objective was the complete entrenchment of his party in power, with the Boer ideals as cardinal principles of government. Malan was out to demonstrate that he, more than Hertzog, was the defender of the Boer way of life. However, he had not yet rallied all the Afrikaners to his banner, and as Hertzog had shown, to do so was the way to permanent tenure of office. Once unity was established, Afrikaner hegemony would be ensured.

To maintain unity and power, all sections of Afrikanerdom had to be given a vested interest in that unity and power. The farmer had to be protected and coddled against flood and drought, against surpluses and losses, and in his ownership of the land. He had to be guaranteed a sufficiency of black labour. The Afrikaans worker had to have a bigger stake in the national prosperity; the 'poor White' element and those who had already been 'uplifted' were to be given tangible proof that their continued prosperity depended on the continuance in office of the National Party. The Afrikaner urban middle-class had to be made secure in its achievements, and Afrikaner enterprise in industry had to be encouraged and capital mobilized among Afrikaners. Each section would have something to lose if the National Party lost power; each section had already begun to taste, under Hertzog, what it might yet gain provided there was continued unity.

In 1948 there were still thousands of Afrikaners supporting the Smuts policy of conciliation, and Dr Malan's party was a minority party in terms of popular votes. But the National Party played continuously on the emotions of Afrikaners outside the fold. Emotional blackmail became a widely-used instrument because there was a danger that with urbanization, Afrikanerdom might lose its grip on some of its people. The Afrikaner culture and way of life was essentially rural and racial, and changes and adaptations were necessary to keep a hold on the city dwellers. It was not enough to make Afrikaners materially dependent — another party with another ideology might also do that. They had also to be emotionally bound to Afrikanerdom. In any country, urbanization breaks down rural traditions very quickly. The dangers to Afrikanerdom were especially acute.

Dr Malan's National Party had no intention of risking electoral defeat, and, electorally, there were a number of threats to its security. Dr Malan could count on seventy-nine Assembly seats and Smuts on seventy-one. There were three White 'native representatives', and in 1946, the Smuts Government had introduced legislation providing for representation of the Indians by three Whites. Elections for these three seats were shortly to be held, and this would have meant a *bloc* of six seats against the Government.

93

The Government would have been reduced to a majority of two. On top of this, the coloured people of the Cape still voted on the common roll. They supported, or would be driven by unfolding Nationalist policy into supporting, the United Party. They were concentrated in constituencies which were closely contested, and in which they held the balance of power.

The programme of ensuring against electoral defeat included a number of measures to counter these threats. Its cornerstone was, of course, the unloading of rural seats.

It is now clear that the Government carried out its programme in different phases and with differing orders of priority. The first priority was to entrench its Parliamentary majority. The removal of coloured voters from the common roll — one of the ways of doing this — proved to be a long and arduous task. The process of bringing Afrikaners back into the fold, begun immediately, was also a long-term one, which was entrusted to the Nationalist Party organization.

The extension to more and more Whites of the benefits of White domination did, of course, aid the Party's work, but it had another effect as well. It meant the increasing curtailment of the rights of Africans, Indians and Coloureds. And of course, the more numerous the infringements of the rights of these human beings, the greater would be their resistance, thus necessitating still further curtailment of their freedom. Malan anticipated this; he started out with the traditional Afrikaner conviction that the White man must dominate or be dominated, and as the ability of the Opposition to oust the Government by electoral means receded, the Government was able to deal with its second priority: the suppression of African resistance.

One urgent matter connected with both these priorities was the loyalty of the armed forces. The Nationalists' refusal to participate in the two world wars had made them indifferent to the defence force, which developed a 'South African' orientation rather than an Afrikaner one. With great thoroughness, the Minister of Defence, Mr F. C. Erasmus, embarked on a programme of

'Afrikanerization' of the army. There were sweeping changes in the High Command, involving a number of premature retirements of officers, effected, curiously enough, by midnight dispatches, and a number of top officers were bowler-hatted. Between January 1st, 1954, and February 3rd, 1956, a hundred and twenty-two officers of the Permanent Force resigned. At this time the total strength of officers in the standing army was only nine hundred and eighty-seven — so the loss was almost thirteen per cent in two years. Mr Erasmus created a number of Afrikaner regiments with Boer traditional names; he redesigned uniforms and renamed certain military ranks. He created South African military decorations — with strong Afrikaner emphasis — and, in the rural areas, established rifle commandos based on the Boer concept of guerilla fighting. Finally, at the end of 1959, by which time African opposition had demonstrated itself as a considerable force, the Government decided to convert the armed forces from an instrument of defence against external aggression to a weapon designed mainly for the suppression of internal resistance. Their training and equipment were altered accordingly.

In viewing the second phase of the Government's programme — that dealing with African and other minority resistance — it is essential to remember that the Nationalist policies are a logical extension of the Voortrekker policies, and that they are based on Boer beliefs and experiences.

To the Afrikaners, the African is an essentially different and *immutably inferior* person. The most vivid image in their group memory is of a treacherous Dingane; or of a black man plundering a farm in the wilderness; or perhaps of a screaming horde of Zulu impis attacking a handful of Whites in a *laager*.

This image is part of the Boer conviction that the African, as a heathen, outside and against the laws of God, is seeking to crush the Boer and to 'drive him into the sea from which he came' — the traditional tribal solution to the White problem.

The second image of the African is a kinder one: of some loyal black servant or retainer, who has been 'Christianized' by the Afrikaner and 'knows his place in life': who has, in fact, accepted the caste system.

The third image is of the educated African and the 'semi-literate barbarian' (as the Afrikaner calls the urban African). In Afrikaner eyes these Africans are the product of the English Christian missionaries and their successors, with their liberal Christian doctrines of universal brotherhood. They are the product of the liberal and humanistic British tradition, and its successors, 'sickly, sentimental liberalism' and Communism. The exponents of these doctrines are the 'agitators' directly responsible for such Africans. It is among these Africans that the creed of African nationalism has taken root; it is among them that Marxist ideas have found some acceptance.

When the Afrikaner states his conviction that Africans must be dominated lest they dominate, his thought is inspired not so much by the fear of African nationalism (which came only later with the liberals and missionaries), as by his group memories of conflict with a 'heathen', 'godless' people, trying to overthrow the Boer and with him the laws of God as he saw them.

The Afrikaner is firm in his conviction that it is necessary — and feasible — to revert to the Boer methods of handling Africans, and that it is possible to eliminate the troublesome, evolved Africans. He believes it possible to convert the African back to the acceptance of the traditional religious teachings of the Boer, to teach him again respect for, servility to, and humility towards the white man. The Afrikaners do not believe — as outsiders do — that they are oppressing the African. They are concerned with the natural, proper and godly order of life, and feel that they are only restoring what has been upset. The black man, says the Afrikaner, can never properly absorb the liberal education given him, because it is against his nature. He can only be made more clever, more cunning and better equipped to overthrow the Boers, who therefore have an added reason to fear him.

The outside observer may see that the greater the oppression, the greater the resistance of the Africans; he may notice that the more the Afrikaner does to allay his fears of Black domination by further oppressing the African, the greater is the likelihood of his fears being confirmed. To a certain extent that realization is dawning upon many Afrikaners. Some of them feel that the choice is now between Afrikaner nationalism or African nationalism, and that they dare give nothing away at this point. To them, the struggle is to the death, and they will justify all that they do in the name of survival. For them, 'necessity constitutes a moral code.'

But many more Afrikaners do not see it that way. To the outside world, experience has shown that a people cannot be kept down for ever; in the experience of the Trekkers it can — and their religion says it must. Only if foreigners introduce alien ideas will the theory fail. In other words, people are not oppressed until someone tells them that they are. Perhaps this is why the Afrikaner has a special hatred for the 'agitator', and his determination to weed out the evolved African is strengthened by fear of him, and of the 'cunning' he has learned from his 'liberal' instruction.

The Afrikaner seeks to dominate by force of law, by military force and by indoctrination of the mind.

Domination is 'an insatiable hunger'. It cannot permit of any concessions. To some, giving way even slightly would be the thin end of the wedge, to others it would mean losing face and undermining the authority of the white man (and therefore also undermining the caste system by which the black man must accept his inferior position). That is why no African in this system can have the vote; to give it would be to equate some black men with Whites.

The economic advantages and privileges enjoyed by the Whites sustain their emotional attitudes to colour. There are laws which prohibit contact between White and Black except as master and servant. They are designed not so much to prevent the breakdown of stereotyped White views of the African as to prevent the African from seeing himself in a manner different from that which the caste system dictates. Moreover, this administrative and legislative protection is a revival of the old Boer idea that manual labour is 'kaffir work', so that Hertzog's hope of preaching the dignity of labour has given way to a policy of advancement of Whites into higher jobs solely on the grounds of their being White. The effect of this on the economy can be imagined.

Territorial segregation came last in the programme of racial domination. It was not until 1959, eleven years after Malan first took office, that any serious thought was given to the matter. It will be remembered that under the Boer republics, Africans lived in locations 'which they held only on good behaviour'.

The Bantu Authorities Act of 1959 was intended to lay the foundations for separate development; to provide an administration for the reserves, which would gradually be given autonomy. These Bantu homelands were intended eventually to 'absorb the total Black population of the Union'. The future course of apartheid, beyond the immediate goals of ensuring White domination, had previously never been clearly defined. What the word meant depended rather on who was dreaming or talking about it. Dr Malan and Mr Strijdom both held office at a time when the immediate task was to secure White domination and entrench the Afrikaner Government in power. By the time Dr Verwoerd became premier, much of the fortress was already built.

Apartheid is said to have 'positive' and 'negative' aspects. Negative apartheid means securing, entrenching and guaranteeing White supremacy; positive apartheid is supposed to mean the political and economic development of the African reserves. Apartheid as a *political theory* was conceived by men of integrity with roots deep in the history of their people, men and women who were fully aware of the traditional conflict between their own people and the Black people and anxious to avoid clashes in the future. To do this, it seemed necessary to avoid economic competition between the races and contact between them, yet impossible to keep every black man permanently a servant. The result was a philosophy of 'separate development' of each group 'along its own lines', which was not without its elements of justice.

But today we find two schools of thought. There is the politician's concept of apartheid and there is the concept held by the high-minded people who are found in Afrikaans universities, in the churches and among leaders of industry, commerce and the professions. The South African Bureau of Racial Affairs has gathered together these high-minded people, whose view is that the African reserves must be intensively developed, politically, agriculturally, culturally and industrially, so that they can absorb the maximum of the Union's Black population, thereby reducing the contact between White and Black.

The vexed question of the political, cultural and economic development of the reserves has been the subject of much controversy between the two main schools of thought, as well as within each. The Nationalist Party has made clear what 'political and cultural development' is to mean in these reserves, and has already rigidly prescribed the pattern. Administration must be in accordance with 'traditional tribal custom' *as conceived by the Government*. The competence of the tribal authorities is strictly limited to matters of local government, and even these powers are subject to continual government checks. Education and cultural development must be within the framework of the Bantu Education and 'Extension' of University Education Acts. The emphasis is on tribalism, and on servility and subservience to the white man.

The character of the subservience that Bantu education is meant to inculcate may well alter with circumstances and may not always simply mean servility to each and every white man. The theory of apartheid envisages a temporary state of affairs in which there will be a large number of black men in White areas, but it is assumed that more and more of them will return to the Bantu homelands and the number will decrease rapidly. Meanwhile, so long as black men are present in the cities, the caste system must be perfected and the master-servant relationship re-established. As the urban Black population decreases and contact is reduced, the subservience must become more general in its

nature. It is not to individual Whites that the Bantu must doff
the hat, but to the White race. He must then accept that the white
man must decide where he shall live, the extent of land on which
he shall live, the nature of government under which he shall live,
the kind of education he shall have and what his culture will be.
To aspire to the Western way of life and to Western democratic
government is not for him; to desire to live in the White urban
areas which his labour has helped build up and to want more land
is also not for him. The subservience is no less real because it means
obedience to the *diktat* of the white man *as a species* rather than
to white men as individuals.

Some of the people of the South African Bureau of Racial
Affairs (SABRA) have begun to realize the danger of a growing
African nationalism. Here is the modern threat to the Afrikaner.
It can, they believe, be dealt with only by an intensive and rapid
political and economic development of the African reserves, whose
autonomy must be established and rapidly expanded. But they
and the Government have not been at one on policies concerning
the African reserves. Many of them have felt that the Government
was going too far in establishing White supremacy, and was guilty
of excess in implementing negative apartheid.

For the person we might call the thinking Afrikaner — he who
feels that we are past the point of no return — the future looks
tragic. He now sees African nationalism as an inevitable force
and feels, perhaps, that his realization has come too late. He has
at last perceived that domination also evokes in the dominated the
desire to dominate. He no longer has an active choice in his political loyalties; he can and will do nothing to weaken Afrikaner
domination, because that will now, in his view, mean the replacement of White supremacy by Black supremacy. He has perhaps
realized that the old Boer idea that the Afrikaner had *ab initio* to
dominate or be dominated was false; he has perhaps finally
accepted that White hate and oppression have bred their counterparts among Africans, that the 'agitator' is not responsible for
African resentment, but that 'oppression' is.

Now he is trapped; he must destroy or be destroyed. Some of those who have thought this out have accepted even the tragedy that faces them and accepted it as Calvinists. 'What we have done already is God's will. Where it finally takes us will also be God's will. We can continue only as God has ordained it.' Indeed, the catharsis is part of the tragedy. Others have taken the plunge into criticism of the Government — and also into isolation, ostracism and the political wilderness.

* * *

The Nationalist policy as I have outlined it has unfolded under four prime ministers. Malan succeeded Smuts chronologically, but as a Nationalist he had succeeded Hertzog. Hertzog had balked at some of Malan's goals, but moderation had to make way for extremism. Malan, in his turn, had mellowed and matured. During the conflict between the Government and the courts over the removal of coloured voters from the common roll (an outline of this appears later), he became reluctant to push it to a conclusion. He also decided that the system of native representation could stay, and before his retirement he made it clear that he wished his successor to be Mr N. C. Havenga, Hertzog's old follower. The Party wanted the more extreme Strijdom, and even he looked moderate when compared with the man who was to succeed him, Dr H. F. Verwoerd.

CHAPTER V

ALL MANNER OF SERVICE

And they made their lives bitter with
hard bondage, in mortar, and in
brick, and in all manner of service . . .
EXODUS I, 14.

L ET us now try to substantiate the charge that the National
Party Government in the Union of South Africa is seeking
to entrench the absolute and exclusive control by the
Afrikaner people of the public life of the land, and to return to the
Voortrekker past.

* * *

When the Nationalists came to power in 1948, Afrikanerdom's
top priority was to ensure that it kept its hold on its people, who
were subjected to the alien influences of modern city life. In his
speech at the inauguration of the Voortrekker Monument in December 1949, Dr Malan, speaking with masterly oratory, said:

'As a result of the urbanization of our people, Afrikanerdom has for the greater part lost its sheltered position,
spiritually as well as economically.
'European poverty, coupled with non-European upliftment, as well as manifold daily contact in every sphere and
on more or less an equal footing, make the struggle for race
purity increasingly difficult. Family life, and with it also religion and morals, gradually break down.
'On the Appian Way, at the entrance to Rome, stands

what is called the Quo Vadis Church. The legend connected with it is that this is the place where Saint Peter, fleeing from persecution and a threat of a martyr's death, met the Lord in a vision bearing His Cross, whom he was on the point of disavowing for a second time.

' "Quo Vadis?" asked the Lord.

' "I am fleeing for my life," the disciple replied. "But quo vadis?"

'Then followed the reply of the Lord: "Now that you are disavowing me a second time, I am going to Rome to be crucified for a second time."

'Peter immediately turned back to allow himself to be crucified for his Lord.

'This monument stands here to the memory, and as a tribute, to the Voortrekkers. But it stands here on the Road of South Africa also for you and your descendants. This is your Quo Vadis shrine ...

'Afrikaner, now and throughout all the future generations! if you have strayed from the Voortrekker spirit and thought, if you have by deed disavowed and again crucified the Voortrekkers to whom you are paying tribute today, and if your eye falls on this monument where you and the Voortrekkers are meeting face to face in spirit today; if that soul-searching question then occurs to you — Afrikaner, quo vadis? — then pause and turn back!

'Back to your people; back to the highest ideals of your people; back to the pledge which has been entrusted to you for safekeeping; back to the altar of your people on which you must lay your sacrifices, and if it is demanded from you also yourself as a sacrifice; back to the sanctity and the inviolability of family life; back to the Christian way of life; back to the Christian faith; back to your Church; back to your God.'

Dr Malan hardly needed to add 'back to the National Party': the rest of the speech shouted it.

Since the first world war, many Afrikaans 'breakaway' societies and organizations have sprung up in the cities, and in all spheres of life the Afrikaner began to establish his own separate counterparts of existing bodies. He withdrew into his own Red Cross (Noodhulpliga); his own boy scout movement (the Voortrekkers); his own chambers of industry and commerce; his own youth organizations, teachers' organizations, women's societies and cultural organizations. In the sense that they all worked for Afrikaner unity and separateness, these organizations served the objectives of the Nationalist Party.

The ideal of Afrikaner unity was also exploited in business. Insurance and investment companies, like Saambou (Build Together), a bank, Volkskas (The People's Bank), and mining and other companies were founded.

Lurking somewhere in the shadows behind the Nationalist Party was the sinister Broederbond (Brothers' Bond), a powerful secret society — a sort of Afrikaans Freemasonry. The Dutch Reformed Church began missionary work in the urban areas — a task made easier because the Afrikaners, like any racial group, tended to live in colonies in the towns and cities. Newspapers were established in the urban areas, and have, over the years, acquired considerable circulations. Moreover, since Dr Malan had in his time been a minister of the Dutch Reformed Church, it was inevitable that there should be some cordial relationship between the Church, or at least vast numbers of its members, and the Nationalist Party which was so true to the Trekker ideals. Certainly the race policies of the National Party have time and again had official support from the Church.

South African education is controlled by the provincial administrations. Because there are two official languages, disputes have arisen over which language shall be used for instruction. There have been some dual-medium schools in a few areas, with instruction in both English and Afrikaans. But the Nationalists, with political control over three of the Union's four provincial councils, have laid down a policy of mother-tongue instruction. This has meant the establishment of specially separated Afrikaans- and English-language schools, and the right of a parent to decide on the language of instruction for his children has been arrogated to the provincial directors of education. In the Afrikaans schools, the policy of Christian National education is being applied to achieve political objectives. The Nationalists have openly justified this policy as a means of capturing for Afrikanerdom the loyalties of children of parents who had strayed from the fold. In 1959, the Government, hoping to collect the political dividend of its education policy, gave the vote to eighteen-year-olds.

There are four Afrikaans-language universities — Stellenbosch, Pretoria, Potchefstroom and the University of the Orange Free State. Afrikaans higher education does not depart from the basic themes of Afrikanerdom in the study of history, religion, culture, etc. 'Culture' means the Afrikaner tradition, and 'history' means the history of the group struggling for its existence 'at the foot of the Black continent'. Other things are taught, of course, but they are critically examined and sifted for inconsistencies with the Afrikaner view of truth. The philosopher must still progress above the level of knowledge, perception and awareness of the ordinary people, but his search and thirst for knowledge must be bounded by the limits prescribed by a potent patriotism.

Finally, the Nationalist Party has exploited the Afrikaner hankering after the old Boer republics. In October 1960, majority approval for a republic was obtained, and the republic was inaugurated in May 1961.

* * *

The post-war Nationalist Government was at first in a precarious position. It had a majority of five and the prospect of seeing this shrink when the three Indian representatives promised by the outgoing Smuts Government were elected. It was, in any case, anathema that Indians should have representation in Parliament, as it might concede the principle that the Indians belonged in

South Africa whereas repatriation was then still the traditional Nationalist policy. In 1949, the representation of Indians provided for in the 1947 Act was abolished. No elections for Indian representatives were ever held.

In the same year, South Africa virtually incorporated South-West Africa. Under the Act of Parliament which effected this, South-West Africa's White population of thirty thousand adults was given six seats in the Union House of Assembly. Less than half the number of voters are needed to send a South-West African M.P. to Parliament as are needed to elect an M.P. in the cities of the Union. The population is largely German, and during the second world war Smuts had alienated it. Malan was sure that he could capture all six seats. He did so, and thus, within two years of coming to power, he had increased his parliamentary majority to ten.

In 1949 the Government introduced the South African Citizen-ship Bill, providing that all alien immigrants must reside in the country for six years before they can acquire citizenship. (Kruger had made it fourteen years before the *Uitlander* could get the vote.) British immigrants had previously been favoured by virtue of reciprocal Commonwealth arrangements and had acquired the citizenship and the franchise after two years' residence in the Union, but now they had only one year's advantage over others, and, like the others, had to conform to certain conditions.

Next the Government pushed ahead with its plan to place the coloured voters of the Cape on a separate voters' roll. Dr Dönges, the Minister of the Interior responsible for piloting the relevant bill through Parliament, said as Dr Malan had said of Indian block representation, that it was an untenable position that the coloured voters should hold a balance of power in a number of seats that were closely contested between the Nationalist and the United Parties. The Europeans, he said, 'realized that the coloured people decided which party was to be elected in a particular constituency'. Although the Act of Union required a two-thirds majority for any amendment of that part of the Act which safeguarded the rights of the coloured voters, the Nationalists argued that this was no longer necessary. The Act of Union had been an Act of the British House of Commons, they claimed, and the Statute of Westminster had since provided that no law of the Commons could have superior force in any dominion to an act of the parliament of that dominion. (After the Statute of Westminster was passed, the Union Parliament itself adopted the Act of Union, thinking this necessary to ensure its continued legality.)

The Nationalists forced the bill to remove the coloured voters through Parliament by a simple majority of the Senate and the Assembly sitting together. Before the passage of the act, the Opposition protested to the Speaker that the Government's procedure was a violation of the Act of Union, but the Speaker decided that the Government could proceed.

A number of coloured voters took the matter to court. The Appeal Court found that the Assembly was not competent to amend the so-called 'entrenched clauses' by a simple majority. The Union Parliament had been created by the Act of Union as a sovereign parliament, but with an inherent limitation upon its powers. It was no less sovereign because it could not remove that limitation by a simple majority; its remedy lay in adopting a specific procedure — that both houses of parliament should sit together, and that a two-thirds majority was required. Certainly, no other power could remove that limitation, not even the House of Commons which had created it.

The Nationalist Government behaved like frustrated litigants. They had been convinced that they were right. They had earlier eliminated the right of appeal to the Privy Council, anticipating that the Appeal Court would find in their favour and that the coloured voters might take the matter further. Dr Dönges asked how 'five old men' (referring to the Appeal Court) could thwart the sovereignty of Parliament. Other Cabinet Ministers referred to the 'dead hand of the past', and the Government resolved that at the forthcoming provincial general elections it would seek a mandate from the people to establish the 'sovereignty of Parliament', in order to place the decisions of the people, as represented in Parliament, above the authority of the courts.

This was the Opposition's finest hour. General Smuts saw the direction in which the Nationalists were going and believed that it was necessary to force a general election before the Government could tamper with the electoral processes by shuffling the constituencies. The most militant part of the 'opposition' was an ex-servicemen's organization known as the Springbok Legion. A number of members of the banned Communist Party sat on the executive of the Legion, and it was, indeed, accused of being under communist control. Smuts had had discussions with members of the executive, and I have been reliably informed that he agreed that if the Legion could arouse sufficient public feeling by mass meetings and demonstrations, he would support them by calling for a complete industrial standstill until the Government agreed to general elections.

The Legion mounted a campaign, but Smuts died before it was properly under way. Torchlight processions were held in the cities and caught the imagination of thousands of ex-servicemen whose memories of the war days were not yet dead. A movement sprang up which became known as the Torch Commando.

As the Torch Commando grew and attracted thousands to its meetings, gatherings and processions, the Government became jittery. But the opposition United Party was also nervous about the growing influence of the Torch Commando. It felt its own authority endangered. It called upon the Commando to drop its call for a general election as its machinery was not geared to fight an immediate election. None of those who survived Smuts had either his stature or the authority to call for an industrial standstill to achieve this objective. United Party leaders met leaders of the Torch Commando and persuaded them to end their campaign, which, they said, might well finish in 'unconstitutional' procedures, for there had already been a number of clashes between police and the Torch Commando.

The Opposition did not realize that the demise of the Torch Commando meant that the power to oust the Government had passed from its hands. The Government may not have fully realized it either at the time, and so, still in fear that it might lose power at the polls, it forged ahead with steps to entrench itself. It was now still more important to ensure that Coloureds were removed from the common roll in the Cape, and that African representation was abolished. Even the judicial setback suffered by the Government was turned against the Opposition. It provided the slogan 'Sovereignty of the People through their Parliament', and it enabled the Government to accuse the Opposition of placing its concern for coloured voters above its concern for Whites.

The steps taken by the Government to remove the coloured voters were spread out over the following three years. Having been rebuked by the Appeal Court for their attempt to by-pass the entrenched clauses of the Act of Union, the Government made Parliament into a 'high court' that could overrule the decisions of the Appeal Court. The Assembly simply passed a law arrogating this power to itself, but the Supreme Court found that this was just a device by which the Government meant to avoid its constitutional obligations. The farcical result was that while the High Court of Parliament at a special sitting in Pretoria was nullifying the Appeal Court's decision, the Appeal Court was finding that the Act declaring Parliament a court was invalid.

Dr Malan decided to abide by the Appeal Court's decision, but a new attack was unleashed on the judges and courts of South Africa. The Nationalist Party won the general election of 1953 with an increased majority, and a 'mandate to establish the sovereignty of Parliament'. In terms of actual votes cast and with allowances made for the respective parties in unopposed seats, the Government was still a minority Government.

The next round in the battle with the courts was to alter their structure and constitution. The Appeal Court had, as a full bench, five judges. It was thenceforth to have eleven, and no sooner was the act passed than new judges were appointed. There can be no doubt whatsoever that some of these judges were either political supporters of the Government or had already expressed the view that the coloured voters could be removed from the common roll by a simple majority. Their appointment was the centre of a great deal of political controversy.

The Government's next step was to alter the constitution of the Senate. Coloured voters could only be removed from the common roll by a two-thirds majority of the Senate and the House of Assembly sitting together. With all other attempts to get round thus frustrated, the Government packed the Senate. There were originally forty-eight senators, elected by electoral colleges comprising the Members of Parliament and the Members of Provincial Council of each province. The four provincial colleges each elected eight members by proportional representation. A further four senators represented the Africans, and twelve were appointed by the Government. The new Senate was to comprise eighty-eight members, of whom twenty-eight were to be elected by the Cape electoral college, twenty-four by the Transvaal, eight by the Orange Free State and eight by Natal. Four would come from South-West Africa, chosen by an electoral college there, another four would be Native Representatives, and the remaining twelve would be appointed by the Government. (Both in the old Senate and in the new, four of the Government-appointed senators were intended to be persons 'who know the reasonable wants and wishes of the native peoples', but earlier governments had set the precedent of not appointing persons who might have voted against them, and reliable government supporters were invariably the beneficiaries of the system.) Under the new Senate Act, the senators elected by the provincial electoral colleges would not be chosen by proportional representation; whichever party held the majority of votes in the electoral college returned all the senators allocated to the province.

In consequence of this contrived arrangement, the Government obtained the necessary two-thirds majority of the Senate and the Assembly sitting together, and the coloured voters were removed from the common voters' roll. When the matter came before the new Appeal Court, it found that the new Senate was legally constituted and had legally, though not necessarily ethically, sat with the Assembly to deprive the coloured people of their rights. Now that the Senate has served its purpose, it has been reduced in size again.

* * *

The entrenchment, extension and protection of White privilege required different measures in the rural and the urban areas. On the *platteland,* racial economic competition was, as I have shown, as old as the first Xhosa-Trekker antagonisms. The measures for dealing with it were the traditional methods that were followed by all the governments chasing the electorally favoured rural vote. Urbanization came much later and its problems were newer.

Not only are the Africans restricted by law to fourteen per cent of the land, but not all of it is personal freehold, and indeed much of it is tribally owned. Today, thirty-two per cent of the African population is still living in these reserves, and another thirty per cent works on White farms. To ensure a sufficiency of cheap farm labour, it has been necessary to prevent African labour from flocking to the cities. Rural depopulation, involving both Black and White, is a continuing phenomenon. Farmers who cannot or will not compete with urban wage structures would find it difficult to prevent their labour from leaving them if it were not for the pass systems, designed to stabilize the African population in the rural areas and in the reserves. To enter a town or city an African must have employment there, have a permit to enter stamped in his pass book, and a permit to leave the place from which he has come. If he is contracted to a farmer, he must first be released from that farmer before he can obtain employment with another.

The pass system has led to many serious abuses. One was the farm labour scandal. Under this system, numbers of Africans arrested on pass charges were offered release on condition that they indentured themselves to farmers in areas where farm labour was short. If they signed the contracts provided, they disappeared for long periods and were not allowed to communicate with their families. After a Johannesburg attorney, Mr Joel Carlson, had exposed the system, and a number of successful *habeas corpus* applications for relatives had been made, the Supreme Court was highly critical of it.

The entrenchment of White privilege in the towns was for the 1948 Nationalist Government a task of great urgency. The 'poor White' problem had long faced Afrikanerdom and successive governments had taken the side of Whites who faced economic competition with the Blacks. The new Government intensified this policy.

The Native Building Workers Act Number 27 of 1951 was an example of things to come. In the words of Section 10, the Minister (of Labour) 'may make such arrangements as he deems fit to provide for natives to be trained to perform skilled work of *a nature and standard required for the construction of buildings for use by natives in native areas* [author's italics] ... ' In addition, the Minister 'shall determine the maximum number of learners to be trained during any given period'. Section 14 provides that 'no employer ... shall employ a native upon skilled work in the building industry within an urban area, elsewhere than in a native area: in any native area employ a European on any building in connection with which any native is employed on skilled work.'

In the Industrial Conciliation Act of 1956, the principle of 'job reservation' was established for all industry. The Act provided for the establishment of a body to investigate inter-racial competition in the labour force, which could recommend 'the reservation either wholly, or to the extent set out in the recommendation, of work, or any specified class of work, or work other than a specified class of work, in the undertaking, industry, trade or occupation concerned, in the specified area or any portion thereof, or in any specified type or class of premises in the specified area, for persons of a specified race, or for persons belonging to a specified class of such race, *and the prohibition of the performance of such work by any other persons* [author's italics].'

Here was the key to the extension of White privilege, since the Minister of Labour had the power to reserve whole categories of work for any racial group. In so far as the Act has already been applied, the reservations have all been exclusively for Whites.

Allied to this is the Government's policy of non-recognition of African Trade Unions, the provision in the Industrial Conciliation Act for the segregation of Whites and Coloureds in separate trade unions, and finally the prohibition of strikes, for any reason whatsoever, by Africans.

While these measures have put more money into the pockets of White workers, they have kept Africans in a state of dire poverty. The per capita income in the reserves, per annum, is less than fifty pounds. And in White rural areas, although wages vary from place to place (and there are some liberal farmers), the figure is not much higher. In the towns and cities it is a great deal higher, but then so are wants. Strangely enough, it is this extension of African wants that the Government so much resents. The belief is that, seeing what the white man possesses, the way the white man lives, the black man will 'covet' and 'envy' his goods and way of life and desire to share in the general wealth. To the Nationalist Afrikaner this is a dangerous trend, for wants are ever-increasing, and he argues that increasing wants will eventually include political aspirations.

The extent of African poverty was first revealed to most Whites during the Johannesburg bus boycott in 1957. The boycott lasted for several months. Hundreds of thousands of Africans walked every day to and from work, seven or eight long miles, rather than pay the extra miserable penny that had been added to their fares.

Not all the political agitation in the world could have had such an effect if there had not been a real and deep grievance. The boycott was spontaneous and began among the poor and penalized people themselves. It succeeded simply because the people could not afford the extra penny. The bus company had to suspend all its buses on the boycott route, and as the months passed the police used every possible method of intimidation to stop the vast daily walk to work. It continued because the people involved had no option. In the end, a settlement was reached as a result of which the Johannesburg City Council and organized commerce bore the extra cost of the bus fares. Both the Council and the Chamber of Commerce promised that African wages would be increased.

The South African Institute of Race Relations subsequently undertook research into the wage standards of Africans. The findings showed that Africans living on the Witwatersrand, where African wages were higher than in any other urban area (all urban areas being considerably better off than rural), were getting on the average almost eight pounds less per month than the minimum amount necessary for subsistence. For food, clothing, rent, transport, lighting and water, the bare essentials of life, for a family of five, £27. 10s. per month was necessary, and the average income of such a family was £18 per month. The difference was somehow made up by most families on next month's salary, but this poverty contributes to illicit liquor brewing, prostitution and crime.

These figures have been officially accepted by the national wage determination board, but the chairman has argued that wages cannot be increased except in conjunction with a rise in productivity, because otherwise the purchasing power of the currency would be debased, necessitating all-round increases for White and Black; in other words, inflation. This argument overlooks a number of factors. First, the productivity of any man will be restricted if he is poorly fed and concerned with the poverty of both himself and his family. Second, the cheap labour policy followed by many employers must be eliminated and employees properly trained. Job reservation and state policy are handicaps. Third, African productivity has in general been increasing everywhere, but the real beneficiaries have been White entrepreneurs and workers. The policy of 'upliftment' of the poor Whites has consistently been followed, very often without regard to their productivity, with the result that, in general economic terms, African productivity has had to be increased to prevent the loss of their purchasing power.

Africans cannot strike for higher wages, and, being denied the vote, can exercise no influence on the state to alter the position. In the Union today, we have the curious spectacle of organized commerce imploring the state to enforce African wage increases. Many employers have taken the initiative and done so themselves, but there are always unscrupulous people who take advantage of situations like this to undercut the prices of their competitors.

Generally speaking, in the present context of South African racialism, any increase in Black wages will lead to White demands for higher wages. The average white man holds the difference to be the measure of his superiority and any narrowing of the gap seems to him to reflect on that. This is so, quite apart from the fact that an increase in African wages unaccompanied by a rise in productivity would necessitate an increase of White wages. But in fact, a rise in African wages, by eliminating some of the poverty, would automatically mean a rise in productivity. Those who argue that the productivity rise must come first or else purchasing power would be debased are simply looking for arguments to keep down Black wages, knowing full well that Whites will expect the increases on political grounds. That is the real factor which increases the cost of living. (See Appendix.)

* * *

Perhaps the most ambitious part of the Government's programme is its plan to 'close the ring' of the caste system; to fashion anew the thinking of the Africans, to bring them back to an acceptance of the subordinate place that their ancestors had been made to tolerate under the Voortrekkers.

This meant a return to the past. It meant controlling the education of Africans and reducing the influence of the 'liberal' Christian missionaries. If the aims of their policy could be achieved, White South Africa would finally be secure within her own borders.

The man for the task was Dr H. F. Verwoerd, who became Minister of Native Affairs in 1949. Before and during the war he was sympathetic towards Nazism in Germany. He had first-hand experience of it as a student in Germany; he was a racial purist, a theoretician, a professor of psychology, hard-working, and above all, a sincere fanatic. He set about bringing Bantu education under his control. The Bantu Education Act provides that *all* education of Africans shall be under the control of the state, and that all schools not maintained by the state itself must be registered with it, and should therefore conform with state policy. Section 9 of the Act provides that registration of a school 'may be refused if the *Minister is of the opinion* [author's italics] that its continued existence is not in the interests of the Bantu people ... ' It is of course, an offence for an unregistered school to continue. Some indication of the Minister's opinion was provided by Dr Verwoerd himself in his speech in Parliament when the Act was introduced.

Apart from refusing registration, the Minister may close any school if he believes that 'its continued existence is not in the interests of the Bantu people ... or is likely to be detrimental to the physical, mental or moral welfare of the pupils or students ... '

The Minister controls not only the schools and their teachers, but the teachers' educational institutes, and, as will be seen later, the 'Bantu universities'. The Minister has the 'power of appointment, transfer, promotion or discharge of teachers' at Bantu schools.

There are certain subjects for which the syllabuses are the same in White and Bantu schools. But the curriculum at Bantu schools is restricted in its scope and uniform for all pupils. Religious instruction, one of the principal media for inculcating subordination in the Bantu, has been taken out of the hands of missionaries (a final revenge on Philip, his contemporaries and their successors) and its control vested in the Department of Bantu Education. This has facilitated reversion to the Boer technique and the Boer religious message. A new subject, social studies, is directly concerned with the 'Bantu's place in South African society'.

Secondary education is limited to the four compulsory subjects —Afrikaans, English, the African home language, social studies— and a choice of three subjects from general arithmetic, commercial arithmetic, mathematics, general science, or physical science, Latin, biology, agriculture, arts and crafts, homecraft, woodwork, bookkeeping, commerce, typing or shorthand. Throughout their schooling, all pupils are given religious instruction as a non-examination subject.

An upper limit of £6,500,000 from the national budget has been established for Bantu education. Any excess that may later be required must be met directly from native taxations, even though Africans already contribute directly and indirectly to the national budget. These underpaid people have to provide the finance for apartheid projects which are imposed on them and in whose implementation they have no choice.

In the financial year 1955-6, the Bantu Education account was: revenue £9,008,675, expenditure £7,884,775. Revenue was made up of the fixed appropriation of £6½ million and four-fifths of the 'Native general tax' amounting to £1,966,283; receipts from Bantu schools totalling £60,639; and the previous year's balance of £481,753.

Between the end of 1956 and October 1957, the number of pupils at Bantu schools rose from 1,101,299 to 1,265,000. Of these, seventy-four per cent were in lower primary classes, twenty-three per cent in higher primary classes, and only three per cent in secondary schools.

When the Minister put the Bantu Education Act through

Parliament, he said: ' ... I take full responsibility for the pegging of the subsidy [of the state] to native education at £6,500,000 ... while the European is prepared to make heavy contributions to native education, the native community will have to shoulder their share of the responsibility ... I recognize the value of the mission societies in the history of Bantu education ... But there are also many bad signs, especially at the present time ... it is evidently very essential that at least in respect of certain churches ... their hold on native education should disappear ... *we do want to indoctrinate the teachers (and children) — if we must use that term — with our spirit, and that is the belief that they must serve their own people and they must not think that once they are educated they can leave their own people and seek equality with the European ... the native teachers must be trained in training schools under our control* [author's italics] ... '

Speaking to the Senate on the subject of Bantu education on June 7th, 1954, Dr Verwoerd added: 'The Bantu teacher must be integrated as an active agent in the process of the development of the Bantu community. *He must learn not to feel above his community, with a consequent desire to become integrated into the life of the European community* [author's italics]. He becomes frustrated and rebellious when this does not take place, and he tries to make his community dissatisfied because of such misdirected ambitions which are alien to his people.'

Control of African lower school, higher school and teachers' institute education would not be effective so long as some Africans could pass on to universities where they would acquire liberal ideas. University education too had to be brought under the control of the Department of Native Affairs. The extension of University Education Act was passed in 1959.

It provides for the establishment of separate universities to serve the different colour groups and African tribes, and for the prohibition of students of one race or tribe (among Africans) from attending a university reserved for another race or tribe. Under the Act, the admission of non-White students to White universities ceased, and Fort Hare College became a Xhosa university for Xhosas only. New tribal universities are being built for other tribal groups. It is a crime for a university to admit a student from a race or tribe other than that which the university is intended to serve, and a crime for the student to enter a university not intended for his race or tribe. The language of instruction is the language of the tribe, and in history and culture the emphasis is on the tribe's progress and past.

The Minister of Bantu Education has complete control of the teaching staff of the Bantu universities. It is he who appoints their senates and councils; it is he who has the 'power to appoint, promote, transfer or discharge' staff, and he 'may refuse admittance to any student if he considers it to be in the interest of the university college concerned to do so'. The councils of the colleges established under the Act must be all White.

Under the original draft of the Act, lecturers would have been guilty of an offence if they had publicly commented adversely upon the administration of any department of the Government or propagated any idea or taken any part or identified themselves with any propaganda or activity or acted in any manner calculated (i) to cause or promote antagonism among any section of the population ... and (ii) to impede, obstruct or undermine the activities of any Government Department.

The Act, as passed, does not contain these provisions. Instead, it places university staff under the Public Service Regulations. It amounts to the same thing. The cost of establishing these universities is to be met from the Bantu Education Account.

Mr Strijdom, then Prime Minister, said on April 5th, 1957, that the 'state could not allow universities to spread doctrines perilous to the life or future of the White race. It is the duty of the state to guard over the nation in this connection and to act as it would in the case of a war to protect the safety of the nation.'

The Minister of Bantu Education, Mr Maree, dismissed seven White members of the staff of Fort Hare soon after it came under his control. He said at a Nationalist Party meeting at Glencoe on

October 2nd, 1959: 'I dispensed with their services because I will not permit a penny of any funds of which I have control to be paid to any persons in these institutions [the new African 'universities'] who are known to be destroying the Government's policy of apartheid, which is what was going on in this instance.'

The Bantu Authorities Act is closely related to the Bantu Education and 'Extension' of University Education Acts. Its methods are, however, different. The purpose of the Act is to re-establish the tribal traditions and loyalties of the Africans 'adapted by the Government to modern circumstances'. If the direct aim is not to divide and rule, it is certainly an extremely important incidental objective. The tribal authorities are to provide the local administrations in the various tribal reserves, with absolutely no contact whatsoever between one large tribal group and another — say, the Zulus and the Xhosas. This is Kruger's policy, the policy of the Trekker republics. The tribal administrations are intended to develop into 'governments' with a 'certain degree of autonomy'. In the cities, where there is ethnic separation (under the Group Areas Act), there are to be representatives of the various tribal administrations to maintain the links between urban 'tribesmen' and their 'governments'. They are to concern themselves with the wants and the grievances of these urban 'expatriates'.

The Act provides for three grades of Bantu authority. At the bottom of the scale, there is the tribal authority; at the next level, a regional authority for two or more areas with established tribal authorities; and finally, a territorial authority for groupings of regional authorities. These groupings are only possible with closely related clans, tribes and sub-tribes.

The chiefs, headmen and councillors of every authority, regardless of level, all hold office at the Minister's pleasure. Regulations prohibit chiefs from belonging to or participating in the activities of any organization 'deemed subversive by the Minister', and the Minister has in several cases already exercised his powers of deposition of chiefs. Headmen or chiefs who refuse to 'comply with any provision of the regulations, or disobey a lawful command given by an authorized officer of the Government' can be dismissed. Both regional and territorial authorities may make by-laws within their respective, closely defined areas of competence, but these by-laws must have the Minister's approval. There are thus checks at every point on the power and limits of the Bantu authorities, even though these authorities are allegedly to provide the basis of government of the Bantustans — or tribal states. Finally, because it was opposed to tribalism, the Bantu Authorities Act abolished the 'Native Representative Council', which, unsatisfactory and powerless though it was, was fairly representative of African opinion.

* * *

The Group Areas Act enforces total residential segregation of the races in the cities; it also prohibits Indians from trading in other than Indian racial areas (thus crippling them economically); and keeps apart African tribes within African townships (according to the law of divide and rule).

The rapidity of urbanization made any kind of town planning almost impossible in many cities; and over the years white and coloured people came to live as close neighbours, while African townships sprang up alongside Afrikaner or other White suburbs. The Group Areas Act, introduced in 1950 and amended many times since, provided for complete residential and other segregation of all the races in urban areas. Reserved areas for Whites, Indians, Coloureds and Africans are being proclaimed, and the Africans, furthermore, are to be channelled into different areas according to their various ethnic and tribal groups. Residential segregation is part of what has often been called the 'traditional South African way of life'.

The Group Areas Act provides that group areas shall be imposed on every urban area. A group areas board, after hearing the evidence of all concerned, decides on the various areas, after which it becomes illegal for persons of one group to live or trade in an area reserved for another group. Churches, schools, mosques, restaurants, temples, cinemas, sports grounds — everything is affected by this, once the areas have been fixed. Compensation is assessed by group areas board valuators. I have, as Liberal Party organizing secretary, been witness to a number of cases in which the valuations placed on properties have been scandalously low. Appeals may be made against the valuations, but this is an involved procedure about which there is a great deal of ignorance among the unfortunate non-Whites who have been affected. And of course it is usually the non-Whites who suffer, since, not being voters, it is naturally they who are moved.

According to the theory of apartheid, the Blacks must return to the reserves where they can develop along their own lines, where they will provide no threat to the white man's way of life and his job, and where they can rise to the highest positions because they are not blocked by white men. South Africa has seen little of this theory applied in practice, and at the moment the Blacks are still necessary for the urban labour force — urban industries are part of the country's life-blood; but they must not be allowed to *gain the impression* that they are a permanent part of the town and city population. When they are moved to residentially segregated areas, they can have no freehold rights (they are allowed thirty years' tenure), for otherwise the Government fears they would regard themselves as something more than temporary sojourners. It seems to be necessary to the philosophy of domination to give the African a sense of insecurity.

Some short while after a start was made in applying the policy of 'ethnic' or tribal segregation in the African townships, serious rioting broke out in Johannesburg 'native locations'. The Government, called upon to appoint a commission of inquiry, refused. The Johannesburg municipality decided to appoint its own. It invited the retired Chief Justice, Mr Centlivres, and two other ex-judges to sit on the commission. These three men found that one of the most important causes of the rioting was ethnic segregation, which had revived tribal loyalties and hostilities.

The determination of the Government to apply its native policy in the face of all opposition is illustrated by two separate instances. In the first, it ignored and by-passed the Johannesburg Municipal Council; in the second, it bullied the Council into submission. When the Government decided to remove the inhabitants of Sophiatown, an African township bordering on a predominantly Afrikaans working-class suburb, the Johannesburg municipality refused to co-operate. The Government immediately set up its own local authority to do the job — the 'Natives Resettlement Board' — which has efficiently removed (and liquidated) the remains of Sophiatown. On the second occasion, the Government threatened to withhold African housing subsidies from the Council if it refused to conform. The Council capitulated. It has agreed to apply the Government's native policies, including ethnic separation, which the Council's own commission of inquiry has found to be the cause of rioting.

To be fair, the housing programme undertaken by this Government must be mentioned. A number of new schools and hospitals have been built; the Nationalist Government has put more African children into schools than any previous Government; it has carried out extensive social welfare programmes. It is not *despite* its native policy that the Government has done this; on the contrary, it is because of it. The Nationalists have set out to revert to their past ideal, and they want their Uncle Toms to live in neat, clean cabins. They do not hate Africans who conform to the pattern they set for them; indeed, they have a cordial regard for such men. But they are determined to break the agitators who create the men who deviate from the pattern. Thus the new housing does not have the freehold rights of the old; it divides the people into tribes; it is further out from the cities; and the rents are higher. The new schools teach 'Bantu education', designed to keep the people servile.

Sophiatown was destroyed because it had become a mixed community, with Indians, Coloureds, Chinese and Africans living side by side. It was destroyed, perhaps, because these people had learned to live together in peace. Sophiatown represented the emergent African, detribalized, living beside people of other tribes in peace and friendship, a product of an industrialized and urbanized modern society. It had acquired a modern character; it was what one calls 'alive'. It produced modern prose, poetry and music of its own. Some of its peoples wrote about the emergent African. Can Themba portrayed the clash between the new and the old Africa. The traditional music was blended with modern jazz, producing novel and lovely sounds. Sophiatown and what it stood for was the antithesis of the Bantu authorities and the Government's directive of 'back to tribalism'.

The removal of Sophiatown was an act of vandalism. It was not only Sophiatown that had to be destroyed, but the way of life that it represented. The township has been replaced by Meadowlands, with row upon row of identical houses, all in long straight lines stretching for miles, this way and that way. Vertically straight and horizontally straight, straight up and down and straight across. To escape the soul-destroying effect, the people who live in these houses have tried to make their houses look different. They have painted the doors and windows in gay colours, or perhaps planted a tree, or started a garden or built a step of red ochre in front of the door. Sophiatown was a slum and it was overcrowded. But it also contained scores of presentable houses, and it represented an emergent Africa on the march.

Africans did not oppose slum clearance but the things that the destruction of Sophiatown stood for and put up a massive struggle against the removal. The Government has therefore been determined to make a success of Meadowlands. The administration is more tolerant there than elsewhere; it is easier for the Africans to get things and to get things done. In Meadowlands there is paternalism, the incentive to conformism. For failure to conform there will be terror and intimidation. Terror like the horror of Sharpeville.

* * *

Other measures passed by the Nationalist Government include the Separate Amenities Act, which provides that the separate facilities established for White and non-White need not be equal. Inferior facilities may legally be made available for non-Whites. Indeed, there is no obligation to make facilities available to them at all.

The Native Laws Amendment Act is designed to prohibit certain kinds of contact between White and Black. Its most repulsive provisions are those which empower the Minister of Native Affairs to prohibit social contact between Whites and Africans and to preclude Africans and Whites from worshipping in the same churches. The Act's main application is to urban areas.

The number of Whites who do have social contacts with Africans is limited. For the Government, the danger of these contacts is their possible effect on Africans. If even a few white men treat Africans as social equals, that would, the Afrikaner nationalists think, undermine the Government's attempt to re-establish the master-servant relationship which was the ideal of the Voortrekkers. Legislation restricting the right of white men to enter 'native reserves' and townships, except by permit, is another way of preventing this.

Racial prejudice becomes ugliest when sex is involved. It is no more than to be expected that sexual contact of Black and White should be outlawed in South Africa. The suave Dr Dönges, Minister of the Interior, piloted the Mixed Marriages Prohibition Act and the Immorality Act through Parliament, saying: 'The object [of these Acts] is, as far as possible, to check blood mixture, and as far as possible promote racial purity. It is an urge born in the South African, Afrikaans- or English-speaking. Now I could say that notwithstanding that urge for the preservation of racial purity, among our people there are weaker brothers and sisters, and a measure of support must be extended to them. They must be protected against their own frailty.'

The poor Whites, of course, were the frontier between the European and the Native. Through their weakness might pour

the 'debasing stream of uncivilized blood'. If any white man suc-
cumbs, the theory goes that it is not only himself he prostitutes, but
his race. He has betrayed the ideal of racial purity and allowed the
thought to spread that white men *do* consort with Blacks; it is a
thought that, if perpetuated, could lead to demands for equality,
and besides, it increases the numbers of the potential 'enemies of
the people'.

The Nursing Bill, introduced in 1957, provides that 'anyone who obliges or permits a White nurse to work under a
non-White person in any hospital or similar institution shall be
guilty of an offence ... ' The Act provides that the Nursing
Council must be an all-White body, with separate advisory boards
for Coloured (and Indian) and African nurses. Separate regis-
ters must be compiled for each race, and different uniforms and
badges can be prescribed for nurses of different races.

Like all the other 'social' apartheid acts, it serves the main
objective to this extent: that it aims at creating an accepted way
of life and thought among all races so that none of them would
ever think of mixing with the others. As new generations are born
and grow up, they will find things thus established and they will
not question the accepted social order and custom. Bantu education, of course, will have given them a correct notion of their
status.

The Population Registration Act of 1950 is designed to classify
people according to race and colour, to sort them out to fit into the
apartheid acts, regulations and administrative measures. If people
are to be administered according to race, there must be an easy
method of knowing which group they belong to, especially in those
borderline cases where Coloureds may appear White or African.

This law requires every man, woman and youth over sixteen
to carry a card of identity. The card indicates by a letter following the identity number the racial group to which the holder
belongs. To arrive at this, human beings in South Africa must all
be examined and classified according to race. The Act provides
for the establishment of race classification boards chaired by

magistrates, to decide — according to prescribed criteria — to what racial group an individual belongs. This has produced count-less instances of hardship, particularly in the Cape. Marriages and homes have been broken because people have had their spouses classified as Coloured. There is no greater slander in South Africa than to call a white man a Coloured.

* * *

If the African, Indian and Coloured peoples could tolerate all the great weight of this oppression, they would be more than human. Their resistance has brought down on them a still greater burden of suppression. Much of the oppressive legislation is also aimed at Whites who join the subjugated non-Whites in their fight.

The first full-scale organized non-White political opposition to the Government since its advent to power was the passive resist-ance campaign of 1952. Known as the Defiance Campaign, its participants deliberately infringed many of the innumerable apartheid regulations. Non-Whites entered post offices through separate entrances provided for Whites; they entered Government buildings and railway stations through the 'wrong' doors; sought service at White counters; sat in the 'Europeans only' coaches in trains, in reserved seats on buses, and waiting-rooms at White railway stations. White supporters used non-White amenities. The campaigners offered themselves peacefully for arrest. Their de-monstrations soon grew in importance.

The Government retaliated immediately by enacting a law against passive resistance or incitement to defiance of any act, ordinance, by-law or regulation, with heavy penalties for infringe-ment, including imprisonment, flogging, fines, or all of these to-gether. At the same time Parliament passed the Public Safety Act, enabling the Government to proclaim a state of emergency and to rule by proclamation. It is that Act, supported in Parliament by the United Party Opposition and passed immediately before the

1953 general election, which the Government invoked in March 1960 to detain almost two thousand political 'offenders' and over eighteen thousand pass and other petty offenders, most of them for well over four months. Not one of the political detainees was subsequently brought before the courts.

African resistance increased with the coming of the Bantu Education Act and the Sophiatown removals. There were mass protest meetings, demonstrations, and, starting in 1956, attempts to call a total work stoppage for short periods. The Government's armoury of repressive measures was already well stocked, but new weapons were introduced with new legislation when necessary.

One of the most restrictive laws in the armoury is the Suppression of Communism Act of 1950. It defines a Communist as 'a person who professes or has at any time before or after the commencement of this Act professed to be a Communist, *or who, after having been given a reasonable opportunity of making such representations as he may consider necessary, is deemed by the Governor General,* or in the case of an inhabitant of the territory of South-West Africa by the Administrator, *to be a Communist on the ground* that he *is advocating, advising, defending* or encouraging, *or has* at any time before or after the commencement of this Act, whether within or outside of the Union, advocated, advised, *defended* or encouraged the achievement of *any of the objects of Communism* or *any act or omission which is calculated to further the achievement of any such object* [author's italics] ... ' The Act empowers the Minister of Justice to declare illegal any 'organization professing to promote the spread of Communism, or propagating its principles or *furthering the achievement of any of the objects of Communism,* or engaging in activities calculated to further' any of its objectives [author's italics].

Later in the Act, there is a definition of Communism: 'Communism means ... and *includes,* in particular, *any doctrine or scheme ... which aims at bringing about any political change ... by unlawful acts or omissions*'; or in another interpretation, 'any industrial, *social* or economic change [author's italics]'. *Unlaw-ful acts are acts against any law of the Government.*

By 1957, the only organization declared illegal under the Act was the Communist Party. As for the 'naming' of persons as 'Communists' under the Act, six hundred persons had been 'so deemed'. This included seventy-six trade unionists, of whom fifty-seven were ordered to resign from their unions. A considerable number of the people 'named' were, or are, avowed Communists, but some of those who were, have since changed their minds.

Some of the other provisions of the Act have, however, been used against persons who are not Communists. It must be remembered that Communist sympathizers in South Africa have for many years been in the forefront of the fight against White domination, at great personal risk, at times with little foreseeable hope, and with great courage. Quite understandably, Africans have not refused their help. But the Government has not confined its actions, under this Act, to non-Communists who accepted help from Communist sympathizers. It has taken action on the wider grounds that opposition to racial domination happens to be one of the objects of Communism. Numbers of people have been prohibited from attending gatherings for periods of five years, or prohibited from entering any area save that in which they are resident. Several gatherings have also been prohibited under the Act.

The best possible comment on the Suppression of Communism Act is that Patrick Duncan, who has been a staunch opponent of Communism in South Africa, and who has consistently used his paper *Contact* to attack it, was himself banned under this Act from addressing gatherings.

The power of the Government to prohibit gatherings, to restrict freedom of speech and to impose some sort of press censorship, as well as the power of banishment (but not of banning individuals from attending meetings) which derive from this Suppression Act, are conferred in other Acts as well.

The power of banishment is given in the Riotous Assemblies Act and the Minister may 'prohibit any person from being within an area defined in [his] notice, whenever *he is satisfied* [author's italics] that such person is promoting feelings of hostility between the European inhabitants of the Union on the one hand and any other section of the inhabitants on the other'.

The same Act empowers the Governor General to 'prohibit any publication or dissemination' of 'any documentary information calculated to engender feelings of hostility ... *whenever it is the opinion of the Governor General* [author's italics] that publication would do this. This Act also confers powers to prohibit gatherings if they are 'calculated', in the opinion of the Minister, to 'engender feelings of hostility'.

Under Section 20 of the Native Laws Amendment Act, 1952, the Governor General *whenever he deems it expedient* in the general public interest' may order *'a tribe'* or an individual African to *'withdraw from any place to any other place, district or province within the Union* [author's italics] and not to return at any time thereafter or during a specified period' without written permission from the Secretary for Native Affairs.

And in 1956, Parliament passed a law providing that when any African has been ordered to leave any area, 'no interdict or other legal process shall be issued for the stay or suspension of the execution of such order ... and no appeal against or review proceedings in respect of such order ... shall have the effect of staying or suspending the execution of such order ... '

Act Number 69 of 1956 gives to an urban local authority the power to banish any African if it is of the opinion that his presence in its area of jurisdiction is 'detrimental to the maintenance of peace and good order'.

The frequent use in conferring power on Ministers or the Governor General of phrases such as 'if he is satisfied' or 'if it is deemed by' or 'if he is of the opinion' has the legal effect of excluding any appeal to the courts.

A new law passed in May 1961 contains a provision that in certain cases the Attorney General may decide whether a man shall
be detained for twelve days instead of the former forty-eight hours
before being charged in court. The Minister said he could see
nothing wrong with giving the Attorney General such powers
because he already had powers which were far more drastic.

The Act also places the onus of proving his innocence on a person accused of intimidation tactics. The Minister said in justifica-
tion: 'Only a man who is lingering about bus stops with his little
briefcase and a man who suddenly appears with a knife in his
hand at the door of a peaceful person can explain his own actions.'

A widespread practice of establishing a multitude of administrative courts with far-reaching powers has grown up in South
Africa. In some cases there can be no appeal to the ordinary
courts, in other cases the right of appeal is limited. Dr E. H.
Brookes and Mr J. B. Macauley, in their *Civil Liberty in South
Africa,* say: When it is considered that the officials who give the
rulings are all Europeans, the case of the non-Europeans, and
especially of the Africans, is hard. Almost the whole of the African's
life is now governed by administrative divisions, appeal from
which to the courts has been deliberately denied by Parliament.
There is thus not merely the tendency of the Administration to
stand by its men against outsiders, but the terrible pride of race,
the urgent need that the white man should not "lose face" by being
put in the wrong before the black man.'

The Union Government also has machinery to deal with
citizens who go abroad to mobilize opinion against the country's
race policies. In 1955 the South African Parliament passed the
Departure from the Union Regulations Act. The issuing of pass-
ports is the prerogative of the Minister of the Interior and he may
refuse to issue a passport. He need not give any reason. The Act
provides that no person may leave the Union without a passport
or permit. Permits are given without difficulty to those who under-
take not to return to the Union. One who is vociferously,

eloquently and logically critical of the Government's race policy
may be unable to return to the Union and in leaving he would
have to choose permanent exile.

Africans may not go on strike. If they do they commit a criminal
offence, incurring a fine of up to five hundred pounds, or imprisonment not exceeding three years, or imprisonment without the
option of a fine, or both. Persons who 'incite' or express sympathy
with or support a strike by Africans incur the same penalties.

The operative Act is the Native Labour (Settlement of Disputes) Act of 1953, and in 1958 a number of persons were prosecuted in terms of it for 'inciting' the one-day strike called by the
African National Congress during that year.

The Treason Trial represented an attempt by the Government
to get the courts to pronounce opposition to apartheid as a capital,
treasonable offence. There have already been suggestions from
Nationalist sources 'that the present common law concept of
treason based on Roman-Dutch principles is obsolete'. It should,
they say, be replaced by a new statutory definition aimed at safe-
guarding the security of the state as now constituted under White
rule if threatened by systematic attempts to establish a Black
regime. It is certainly reasonable to assume of this Government
that what it fails to achieve by a court decision based on existing
law will simply be attained by a law that leaves the courts with no
option.

After the events of Sharpeville in March 1960, Parliament
rushed through an Act empowering the Minister of Justice to ban
both the Pan-Africanist Congress and the African National Congress and any other organizations which might succeed them. The
Minister of Justice acted immediately on these powers, which
means that the two most effective organs of African opposition
have now been outlawed.

The Government had earlier threatened to make the advocacy
of boycott, either at home or abroad, a criminal offence, but the

events of Sharpeville disturbed the legislative programme it had in mind and made other legislation more urgent. The declaration of the state of emergency at the end of March 1960 enabled 'emergency regulations' to be proclaimed, with far-reaching powers placed in the hands of the Minister of Justice. These powers included the right of indefinite detention of any person and the prohibition of publication of the names of detainees until such names had been tabled in the House of Assembly. They also provided that advocacy of boycott should be a criminal offence.

In speaking of the various instruments of oppression, I have said very little of the Security Branch of the South African Police, more commonly known as the 'special branch'. It is, in fact, the political branch of the Criminal Investigation Department, and has become ubiquitous in South Africa. Reorganized after the Nationalists came to power, it has become an empire within the police force. I can say nothing authoritative about the special branch, as I am not in a position to do so. My contact with it while I was in the Department of External Affairs was extremely limited (and I am precluded by the Official Secrets Act from commenting on it). What I have to say is based only on my own subsequent contact and brushes with the force, and information that I have received and have no reason to disbelieve.

If it has expanded in size, it has also expanded in authority and its head is in direct contact with the Minister of Justice — bypassing superior officers, including the Commissioner of Police. Indeed, the special branch sometimes operates without the Commissioner's knowledge. Originally it was confined to the larger urban areas, but it has now spread its tentacles throughout the country. Apart from its power to arrest under a mass of oppressive legislation that makes opposition almost impossible, it is directly responsible for recommendations of banning, banishment and other methods of putting people 'out of action'. It also uses intimidation and threats. It visits employers of people seen at meetings and calls on parents or the university authorities about students whose opinions it dislikes. In South African law, an African could, before 1961, be arrested and detained for forty-eight hours without charge and since 1961, for up to twelve days. These powers have often been used to isolate key leaders at crucial moments.

I have myself twice been threatened with assault by members of the branch, and I know of several instances of threats against Africans. There is absolutely no question but that telephones are tapped in South Africa on a massive scale, and that mail is tampered with, opened, and has sometimes disappeared (though this is very rare).

The Liberal Party proved official tampering with mail in 1955. A letter cleared of finger-prints was sealed by a finger-print expert in Johannesburg before a barrister. It was sent to Cape Town and there opened by another expert (again before a barrister). It was found to be heavily finger-printed. On another occasion an envelope containing a letter sent by the Party from Johannesburg was found, on arrival in Cape Town, to contain a letter written by the National Union of South African Students to an international body; the Party's letter later arrived at the headquarters of the international body.

There is a network of part-time informers and spies throughout the country. Some of them are paid by the special branch. Early in 1959, one of these spies, an attractive young woman student at the University of the Witwatersrand, was uncovered by three members of the Liberal Party, two of whom were also student leaders. A few of the African spies are said to be kept going by supplies of liquor from the special branch, and there have been instances in which persons faced with criminal charges have not been prosecuted provided that they would become informers.

Special branch officers are to be seen at every meeting of every organization radically opposed to the Government's colour policies. Periodical raids are made on the offices and the homes of officials of these organizations. Usually, documents and books are seized.

The South African police force as a whole has become an instrument for the enforcement of government race policies, although I have met and heard of some exemplary police officers who are always courteous in the course of their duties. But the force today includes a large number of young men who are, ideologically, wholehearted supporters of the Nationalist regime and have brought into the force the bitter racial antagonism of their kind. Moreover, the earlier, relatively high educational requirements for admission to the force have been relaxed, largely because with increasing competition for better-class White manpower throughout the country, the force has had to scrape the bottom of the barrel.

When Mr C. R. Swart was the Minister of Justice, he took the side of the force whenever it was, for any reason, exposed to public criticism. He steadfastly refused to appoint commissions of inquiry. He argued that the police had constantly to act in dangerous circumstances, and that if their actions were to be subjected to the scrutiny of a judicial commission each time they were forced to use violence, they would feel hampered when exposed to danger. This would increase the risks they had to face. The only occasion on which the Government has ever climbed down on this stand was after Sharpeville, when, having already taken up Mr Swart's position, they were faced with a barrage of world criticism and capitulated. There is a tragic suspicion among those who oppose the Government that the police have been made over-confident by the abiding and comforting knowledge of government support on all occasions, and that very rarely are all other methods of dispersing crowds exhausted before fire-arms are used.

Policemen are frequently charged with assault, especially on Africans. The Minister of Justice has disclosed, in answer to a question in the House of Assembly, that there were in the years 1956 to 1958, two hundred and sixty-two instances of assaults by policemen on Africans; but they were followed by less than ten dismissals from the force.

Further evidence of Government support of the police,

whatever they do, is given by the fact that the Government is indemnifying itself against claims for damages from victims (and dependants of the dead) of the Sharpeville and Langa shootings.

Since the events of Sharpeville, the South African police have been drastically reorganized. There have been changes in the top command, and it seems likely that a new policy will be applied in promotions, with preference being given to Afrikaner Nationalists. The new command's first directive, however, was for greater courtesy to Africans. There was strict insistence that the insulting word 'kaffir' should not be used in addressing them. The directive said that Africans should not, as before, be summarily arrested for failure to produce passes. Mr Swart said early in 1959 that such instructions had been issued, but there was at that time little indication that they were being acted on.

* * *

The main interference with the freedom of the press has been under the Suppression of Communism Act. There is already censorship of imported publications, books or films. The Government also has the power, when a state of emergency has been declared, to curtail press freedom under the Public Safety Act. These powers were used to a limited extent during the invocation of the Act in 1960. It became an offence to publish the names of detainees. The regulations framed under the Act provided for very wide restrictions on the press, but they were, with three exceptions, used as no more than a threat.

Though the Publications and Entertainments Bill which would have prevented the publication of 'any undesirable newspaper' (undesirable, by definition, meaning, *inter alia,* anything which 'prejudicially affects the safety of the state'), has been withdrawn, Dr Verwoerd has disturbed journalists in South Africa by calling for 'self-control' on the part of foreign correspondents. And already a new and only slightly less drastic censorship bill has been foreshadowed.

ALL MANNER OF SERVICE

In general, the Government prefers to keep the press in sus-
pended fear of control and to intimidate rather than actually
control it. Critical foreign correspondents are restricted in various
ways. (It must be admitted that there have been a number of false
and exaggerated reports in the press abroad which are extremely
unfortunate because, if questionable reports are published abroad
and the Government is able to deny them, they make the whole
of a particular journalist's writing suspect to fair-minded people.
These reports are especially unfortunate because Hansard and the
Statute Book are a sufficient indictment of the Nationalists. I do
not believe, however, that the complaints of distortion are in
general justified.)

A press commission was appointed in 1954. It has not yet sub-
mitted its report. It has wide terms of reference, and has, while it
has been sitting, been something of a sword of Damocles hanging
over the press. Certainly, many South African journalists see it
that way.

The comments on press freedom, of the Minister of External
Affairs, Mr Eric Louw are revealing. 'I say, Mr Speaker, that the
time has arrived when steps should be taken to prevent newspapers
from abusing the freedom of the Press, which they enjoy ... it is
certainly not in the interests of White civilization in this country
that a newspaper of repute and standing should give so much
publicity to a movement in Britain for assisting and encouraging
the resistance movement in this country.'

During the 1960 state of emergency, disturbing acts of intimidation of South African pressmen took place. Steps were taken
against at least two journalists. Mr Patrick Duncan, editor of the
Liberal fortnightly *Contact,* was charged with failure to disclose
sources of information to the police under Section 85 of the
Criminal Procedure Act of 1955. This Act provides that where
anyone refuses to answer such questions as are put to him by a
magistrate 'without any just excuse of such refusal ... the Court
may adjourn proceedings for any period not exceeding eight days
and may, in the meantime, by a warrant commit any person so

137

GUILTY LAND

refusing ... to a jail unless he sooner consents to what is required of him.' Mr Duncan was in jail for twenty-four days before his release on the grounds that 'the required information was obtained elsewhere.' Action has been taken against various other journalists for contravening provisions of the state of emergency.

* * *

The South African Broadcasting Corporation has recently been openly used to broadcast propaganda for White supremacy and the Afrikaner nationalist cause. A former editor of *Die Transvaler* (the Transvaal Nationalist newspaper) has been appointed 'cultural adviser' to the S.A.B.C. He presents a heavily-biased survey of the South African scene. When the S.A.B.C. came under fire as a result of these developments, the then Director-General, Mr Gideon Roos, stated that it was the duty of the Corporation to stand by the Government in a time of crisis such as the Union was then entering.

Gideon Roos has since resigned as Director-General of the S.A.B.C. because more and more of his powers were taken over by the S.A.B.C.'s Board of Control, of which the Chairman is Dr P. J. Meyer, appointed for his strong and outspoken Nationalist sympathies. There have been a large number of resignations from the S.A.B.C., which has increasingly become a government propaganda machine.

* * *

Finally, let us look to the future of Afrikaner policy. The 'Bantustan' policy of 'giving the Natives areas in which they can develop along their own lines' has been hailed with much fanfare by the Afrikaners. What is the truth?

It is my own view that these reserve areas have been planned as nothing more than reservoirs of cheap Black labour for farms in White areas. The siting of industries on the borders of the

138

reserves is designed to attract Africans away from the cities. An upper ceiling has been placed on the political and economic development of the African in the 'Bantustans', and both are rigidly controlled by the Government. Africans will in this way be set apart, but their labour will be retained *for the benefit* of the White economy, and *not in competition with it* in dual (or multiple) economies with different wage and price structures.

The facts which are available are these: there is a policy laid down with regard to Bantu school and higher education, tribal government, the extent and location of the Bantu homelands, the denial of freehold rights in urban areas, and there is the pass system controlling the movement of Africans. It has been made more rigid under this government, and passes, which were not previously required by African women, now are. The Malan Government appointed the Tomlinson Commission to examine the feasibility of apartheid, to see whether the native reserves could absorb the Union's Black population, and what the cost of development would be. The Commission sat for five years and produced a voluminous and detailed report. It found that the native reserves could not absorb the whole Black population and that a certain minimum of Africans would have to remain in the urban areas. Reporting in 1956, it recommended that one hundred and eight million pounds would be necessary for the development of the reserves over the next ten years. The Government rejected the Commission's findings that the Bantu homelands could not absorb the Union's whole Black population, and rejected more than three-quarters of the Commission's recommendations. Dr H. F. Verwoerd was then Minister of Native Affairs. He said that the Commission had failed to take into account that the three High Commission territories, Basutoland, Swaziland and Bechuanaland (which are British Protectorates) *must and would be* incorporated in South Africa, and that their potential land area, mineral wealth and other riches had been overlooked. Dr Verwoerd rejected the Commission's recommendation that the cost of development be met from the national budget. The Bantu must pay for their own development, in the Government's view.

Though it was Dr Verwoerd who, as Minister of Native Affairs, rejected the findings and most of the recommendations of the Tomlinson Commission, when he became Prime Minister he was the very man who made all the lavish promises about the Bantustans. It may be that these apparent contradictions are explained by the vagaries of public opinion.

Perhaps public opinion is the real question-mark in the implementation of apartheid. It is difficult to generalize about the political views of the Afrikaner man-in-the-street.

What are the essential points of agreement among them as a people, and more especially as supporters of the Nationalist Party? More than anything else, there is a commonly held view of the African, in its essence the one held by the Voortrekkers. Over the years, in consequence of greater contact, the advent of the urban-educated and semi-literate African as a new substantial class, and increased economic competition, relations between Black and White have deteriorated. What does apartheid mean to Afrikaners as a group? Does it mean the same to both the rural and the urban Afrikaner? Does it mean the same to the Afrikaner worker as to the Afrikaner businessman? They may all have a stake in the unity of their people within their party, but does that mean that they are at one on the implementation of apartheid? The Afrikaner farmer wants Black farm labour; to him, the essential job of apartheid is to give him a sufficiency of it, and the pass laws and African land shortage both do this. To the urban middle-class Afrikaner, apartheid's job is to provide someone inferior to do the dirty work, able to fetch and carry tools and materials, but not allowed to rise above that place. There are those who can justify the subjection of the Blacks in the religious, historical and philosophic terms of the Trekkers, and there are those who are the heirs of earlier opinions without bothering to justify them. The black man is inferior because he is inferior. The black man is dirty and unhygienic and he has a lower standard of living. He is paid less. That is how he is because that is how he is. It is irrelevant to ask whether his standard of living is low because he is paid less. It is simply that he is paid less because his standard of living is low and because he is dirty and unhygienic.

Is it possible to find among all this a common ethical attitude towards apartheid as a means of allowing the African to develop in his own areas? And having found the common ethical attitude, are all the various groups likely to act on it, in the interests of salvation, by making the necessary financial sacrifice? And when total territorial separation results for each sector in the disappearance of the particular benefit which had made apartheid understandable and beneficial to it, will unity be maintained? Is the average Afrikaner interested in the development of the black man whom he regards as inferior and whom he really wants only to convert into the loyal servant of Voortrekker times?

The Nationalists have been in power since 1948, and the time is drawing nearer for positive apartheid to be put into force. The voters must face the financial implications of this, which so far they have not done. Indeed, one wonders whether the Government would have won the general elections of 1958 if it had committed the taxpayers to the costs of carrying out the recommendations of the Tomlinson Report. Since then, events in Africa have been unfolding with remarkable rapidity. The Union's own African population is becoming increasingly restless. Clearly black men cannot be allowed to advance in the White urban areas, since this would make them a threat to the Whites. Development has to be diverted to the tribal reserves.

On becoming Prime Minister, Dr Verwoerd's first concern was to announce the policy of Bantustans. It was the logical extension of the thinking that underlay the Bantu Authorities Act. The Nationalist Press hailed the statement as the Magna Carta for Africans. Dr Verwoerd said that the days of racial discrimination had ended. Nothing would stand in the way of the development of the native reserves into completely independent states. Their future depended on themselves. This was the dawn of a new era in relations between Black and White. The system of Bantu authorities had been so successful, Dr Verwoerd said, that their competence could be widened on the road towards their independence.

The Promotion of Bantu Self-Government Act was immediately passed, to give effect to Dr Verwoerd's statement. It is important to examine what Dr Verwoerd's theory means in practice. The last provision of the Act had the most immediate practical effect. It abolished native representation in Parliament. The three White members of the Assembly elected to represent Africans and the four White Senators given the same task were all unseated.

The Government presented a white paper to explain the Bantu Self-Government Promotion Bill. It was said to make 'provision for the gradual development of self-governing Bantu national units'. The Prime Minister is quoted as saying that 'if the various Bantu national units show the ability to attain the required stage of self-sufficiency, they will eventually form a South African commonwealth together with White South Africa, which will serve as its core and as guardian of the emergent Bantu states.'

Dr Verwoerd's statement promised much. On examination it is seen that the deeds have not matched the words. When Dr Verwoerd said that 'the days of racial discrimination are numbered', he was referring only to the native reserves. He said in his speech that 'it was important to tell the Bantu peoples and the world' that this was our policy. He was speaking that day to the world and to the peoples in the native reserves, who would be the beneficiaries of his policy.

He was therefore concerned with making a good impression on those tribal leaders whose co-operation he needed to win to make his policies succeed. He had just become Prime Minister and leader of the Nationalist Party, and it was the best time to make the right impression. He had, as Minister of Native Affairs, been the cabinet minister directly responsible for much of the oppressive legislation and oppressive administrative measures which curtailed African rights to entrench White supremacy. Now that the bulk of this was already on the statute book, the time was ripe to speak of the positive side of apartheid for Africans. He could appear as the harbinger of the new era. *The effect on the Whites, who heard Dr Verwoerd's startling words, without examining his deeds, was that at the elections held soon after, for the first time since they came to power, the Nationalists failed to make any electoral gains.*

Since then, the Bantustan policy has gradually become clearer. Dr W. W. M. Eiselen, the Secretary for Native Affairs, has written an article in *Optima,* which is published by Mr H. Oppenheimer's Anglo-American Corporation, in which he has made it clear that the Bantustans will *never* have complete independence. This was an apparent contradiction of Dr Verwoerd's declaration that nothing would be placed in the way of their development towards independence. But, asked in Parliament to reconcile the contradiction, Dr Verwoerd denied that there was any. His failure to repudiate Dr Eiselen confirmed the suspicion that there is no intention of granting independence.

Dr Eiselen also dealt with some aspects of economic development of the reserves. There would be no pump-priming, he said, and no White capital would be allowed into the 'reserves'. The Africans would appreciate the development only if they were responsible for it themselves. This is a curious argument, since South Africa's gold-mining and other industries have been so heavily dependent on foreign investment. Dr Eiselen confirmed that it was not the intention of the Government to ask the White electorate to finance the development of the reserves. This, despite the fact that on Dr Verwoerd's own estimate, Africans pay over thirty million pounds a year in indirect taxation.

The Tomlinson Commission recommended the expenditure of one hundred and eight million pounds over ten years for the development of the reserves, and stated that even then they would not be able to absorb the whole of the Union's Black population. In the five years since the report was made fifty million pounds should have been spent. The Government has paid out less than five million pounds. This is a reflection of its earnest in developing the Bantu homelands. Half a million pounds was made available to a Bantu Industrial Development Corporation intended to mobilize African capital. The per capita income of the reserve population is less than fifty pounds per annum. Although the Government originally laid down the policy that Whites, especially traders, must leave the Bantu homelands so that all trading can be in the hands of Africans, the Minister of Bantu Administration and Development said late in 1959 that no White traders will in the foreseeable future be forced to quit.

The Government decided in 1956 that although no White capital investment will be permitted in the reserves themselves, White industrialists will be encouraged to build factories on the borders of the reserves, near to the sources of abundant cheap labour. Education for servility — Bantu education — begins to make sense in this context. The Bantustans are not really to become independent; they are to harbour a docile cheap labour force to serve the rural farmers and the rural industries.

The failure of Bantustan has been proved by the unrest and turbulence in traditional peaceful areas like Sekhukuneland and Zeerust, where Bantu authorities were imposed against great opposition. In June 1960 there were troubles in the Transkei native reserves, where tribesmen opposed Bantu authorities. In Pondoland which falls within the Transkei there was a state of emergency at the time of going to press, continuing unrest bordering on civil war and a ruthless police oppression. A curtain of secrecy fell over all three of these areas during the troubles. These are the 'free' states where Bantu self-government is being granted.

Bantustans constitute a vast superstructure of officials, predominantly White, on highly unsteady foundations of unrest. Bantu authorities consist of numbers of appointed officials uneasily ruling people who resent them.

In mid-1961, the Transkei Bantu Territorial Authority called for independence. The Transkei's call for independence is important only in so far as it exposes the fraud of the Government's

Bantustan promises. The Government has had to manoeuvre itself out of an impossible position by persuading the Transkei territorial authorities to appoint a commission to examine their proposals.

The feasibility of total territorial segregation becomes still more remote as the country's economy suffers the strain of apartheid and the massive drain on foreign reserves.

*   *   *

The real tragedy of South Africa is that many Afrikaners have come round to recognizing that the policies of the Nationalist Government are oppressive, and that the oppression may be responsible for giving African nationalism the goal of dominating the Whites. And having given to African nationalism a goal it never had before, they now feel obliged to stick with Afrikaner nationalism and to press on until one side is finally crushed by the other.

PART THREE

THE WIND OF CHANGE

CHAPTER I

BIRTH OF THE OPPOSITION

WE have seen how Nationalists and Unionists, English and Afrikaners, have helped to create today's situation. Let us now look at one of the more encouraging signs of the genuine opposition, both Black and White.

Although a South African Native Convention was organized in 1909, its main purpose was to press for recognition of African rights in the Act of Union, and the South African Native National Congress, formed in 1912, was the first long-term, co-ordinated and comprehensive political African organization, with four provincial branches meeting annually in national conference.

In 1913, the Natives Land Act gave the new body a considerable shock. Industrialization and urbanization had only begun to effect the great social and economic changes that were to follow, and the question of land ownership was still the most crucial one in the relations between White and Black. That Africans were denied the right to buy land except in reserve areas was felt very keenly by those who were educated and detribalized. But they had a glimpse now of what the future of their people was to be under this white man's Union.

In the 'twenties, after more and more factories had grown up in the cities, Clements Kedalie, an African from Nyasaland, formed his Industrial and Commercial Workers' Union for Africans, which, for a while, overshadowed the Congress of 1912. Its size and success depended very greatly on Clements Kedalie's personality, and its eventual collapse seemed to many Africans to have begun with Kedalie's association with liberal Whites and left-wing White infiltration of the organization.

During the next three decades, racial oppression was intensified.

It affected more and more Africans personally, directly and deeply. African unity grew, and the major African organization, which was still the Congress, was converted into a militant mass movement. African national consciousness emerged from this to become African nationalism. It was nationalism in its broadest sense — as a feature of nationhood.

Unfortunately, this nationalism was soon affected by something else. The more intense Afrikaner domination became, the stronger was African reaction. The early racial prejudices of the Whites towards Africans soon began to be reflected in a certain amount of anti-White feeling. Many Africans began to feel that they could not rely on the White Parliament for their salvation. Indeed, they felt that they would have to seize their rights with their own hands.

It is idle to reflect whether the situation might have been different if the Cape liberal tradition had not died with Union and had become instead the dominant force in colour policies. Would all men then have become equal in a society which did not think in terms of race? Certainly, until the Act of Union, the Africans of the Cape, who produced the greatest number of educated and literate people, were inclined to regard themselves less as a separate entity than as an integral part of a wider community. But the voices that spoke up for the Cape tradition in the years that followed became fewer and farther between in all spheres of life — in politics, in the churches, in higher education, in sport. The northern Boer tradition invaded every sphere of human activity. All political parties from the Nationalists to Labour (and some Communists) paid homage to the colour bar.

The Africans themselves bore the main burden of their fight against racial domination. The odd white man associated himself with them, but this was very much the exception. These isolated souls were remaindered politicians from the Cape, a very occasional cleric, one or two university lecturers, and a few newly-arrived immigrants. There was no articulate liberal movement; indeed, these few White liberals were a brake on any kind of drastic African action.

It was only after the second world war and after the Nationalists returned to power — this time under Malan — that the liberals began to find their consciences. The South African Liberal Party was formed in 1953, to work for a society in which no man thinks of another's race. The Liberal resurrection was a long time in coming: the Communist Party had already been banned. Most of its members were barred by law from doing political work, but a number of the younger sympathizers who had not been known as Communists went into other organizations.

Though the Liberals could claim to represent a tradition that was older than all the others, especially in southern Africa, it was by now very much a faded tradition. The Liberal revival seemed to be born out of the realization that 'domination evokes the desire to counter-dominate', to quote Professor I. D. MacCrone of the University of the Witwatersrand. A hundred years earlier when the missionary Philip preached liberalism and the British enforced it, the movement had truly reflected the desire to give to men what rightly belonged to them. Now the era of racial domination had intervened, and Africans had already accepted the implicit challenge of the racialist doctrine. The challenge was — and is — for them to fight for those rights which are no longer regarded as their due.

The Liberal revival could be interpreted — as it was by many Africans — as a White response to the African counter-challenge. In the circumstances in which Liberalism was reborn, it seemed to some Africans that its prime aim was not so much to give Africans their due as to save the white man from the consequences of his actions. 'Why,' Africans asked, 'are they only now coming to preach against racialism, when we have already been forced to think of ourselves as Africans?' Was it not Liberalism in Britain, they argued, which had delivered Africans into the hands of the Boers?

African politics had long since gone beyond simple protest at the indignities of racial discrimination. They were now concerned with wider social problems and were bound up with African

nationalism as a mass movement. It was no longer a passive reaction to racialism, but an active and positive, militant and
dynamic force, determined to combat White economic privilege
with neo-socialist doctrine. It had abandoned hope in 'parliamentary' change, which the Liberals advocated.

The Liberal Party declared its opposition to 'all forms of totali-
tarianism, such as Communism and Fascism', and it was clearly
not looking for a drastic overhaul of the economic system. Its
aim was simply to remove racial discrimination. But Communism
had taught many Africans that the removal of the colour bar was
not in itself sufficient; an African might then be allowed into an
hotel, but could he afford it? Communists, furthermore, had been
on the African side for twenty or more years; the Liberals were a
small, powerless, mainly White group.

The Liberal Party's membership was open to all races. Despite
the Liberal protestations to the contrary, this seemed to Africans
like competition with Congress. The Party advocated a qualified
franchise with restrictions applying equally to all. This was less
than the Cape liberal tradition had offered a hundred years before
the Party was formed. The A.N.C. was already a mass movement,
representing the thousands of voteless Africans who suffered
directly from the effects of apartheid. The Liberal Party seemed
to want those who failed to conform to its qualifications to remain
voteless.

The Liberals could not, at that time, understand the suspicions
of the Africans. They formed their political party because White
oppression was, in 1953, worse than ever before, and White resistance to the trend at its lowest. The United Party 'Opposition'
was a 'me-too' party, which imitated the Nationalists. Its so-called
liberal wing had capitulated to the conservatives.

The Liberal Party decided to fight racial domination at the
polls. It would rely on logic, argument and persuasion. It frowned
on extra-parliamentary or unconstitutional action. Africans had
long ago tried and exhausted these methods of parliamentary
struggle. This was not then appreciated by the Liberal Party.

But gradually the Liberal Party overcame many African suspicions. It began to prove its good faith. By 1959 it had accepted the need for universal adult suffrage; it had come to believe that extra-parliamentary action was necessary to overthrow White domination, and it had started to involve itself in such action. It was even beginning to accept that changes were necessary in the country's economic system; though in this respect there is still a wide gap between Liberals and the main body of African opinion.

At this time, in August 1959, the 'liberal' wing of the United Party came to the same conclusions as those reached by the Liberals in 1953. They realized that it was impossible to propagate liberal ideas from the bosom of a conservative party — especially when the conservative party was doing its best to look more right-wing than the Nationalists. Thirteen Members of Parliament split from the United Party and became the Progressive Party. Their policy was the same as the Liberal Party's had been at the time of its formation five years previously.

Just as the Liberals came to reach a closer understanding with the African National Congress, the African body began to split. As a 'liberating movement', it would be expected to gather together all those who were agreed on freedom, even while perhaps disagreeing among themselves on ideological grounds. But the differences within the A.N.C. concerned the methods of winning freedom. The Africanist wing of Congress was opposed to alliance with organizations based on other racial groups and felt that only African nationalists could be relied on to get African liberation. They were widely accused of being anti-White.

There are, then, two very different courses of opposition — one inside Parliament and preoccupied with elections — White opposition; the other predominantly outside Parliament — African opposition. For the oppressed racial groups, the White Parliament has, by and large, ceased to hold any hope.

CHAPTER II

AFRICANS AND AFRICANISTS

THE black man has always been involved in the white man's politics, even in the politics of the Afrikaner nationalists. In the beginning, he was only an issue — a subject for discussion. His influence in shaping policy was negative and passive. The white man looked at the African and invented policies in reaction to what he saw. But there has always been a vast power outside the White political arena.

The Native National Congress was formed in 1912 'for the purpose of creating national unity and defending our rights and privileges'. It survived until the fiftieth anniversary of the Union that provoked its creation. Then it was banned. It survived the challenges of bodies which in their time were larger, but shorter-lived. It had its ups and downs. It languished in inertia over long periods, on occasion being roused to action by some drastic Government measure. But its action rarely went further than sending deputations or organizing meetings and congresses.

The year 1943 was the turning-point for the old Congress. In that year the Congress Youth League was founded. In 1944 a young, dynamic man named Anton Lembede became its president and, until his death four years later, its driving spirit. The league aimed 'to rally and unite the African youth into one national front on the basis of African nationalism'.

In 1949 the Youth League adopted a 'Programme of Action' which declared 'its fundamental principles' to be 'inspired by the desire to achieve national freedom. By freedom we mean freedom from White domination and the attainment of political independence ... '

The new campaigners challenged all the old attitudes of

Congress and the 'Old Guard' policies of negotiation and petition. The new weapons were to be boycotts, strikes, civil disobedience and acts of non-cooperation with the authorities.

The African National Congress and the new alliance it formed with representative organizations of the other subjugated racial groups soon confirmed the rejection of the old policy of negotiation and argument with the Whites. It was now ready for 'positive action'. The alliance committed itself to extra-parliamentary and extra-constitutional opposition, although violence was eschewed. So began the passive resistance — or 'defiance' — campaign of 1952. However, passive resistance was soon made illegal, and Congress was forced to find new kinds of positive action. For two or three years following the passive resistance campaign, its main preoccupation was with meetings and demonstrations, until, following the spontaneous bus boycott early in 1957, it decided to call a one-day strike of all non-White workers. The strike was a moderate success, and the same tactics were repeated the following year. This time the strike was to last three days and was to take place while the white man was voting at the general election. It was an unqualified failure, and a number of leaders were prosecuted for incitement to strike. In mid-1959, Congress launched its campaign of boycott of Nationalist goods.

Meanwhile, the Congress movement defined and declared its objectives. It demanded universal suffrage, although it declared itself opposed to a narrow or sectional nationalism. The most powerful exponent of this policy was ex-Chief Luthuli, who said repeatedly that Congress stood for a broad South African nationalism.

In 1955, Congress had called a mass conference of many organizations in Kliptown, a largely coloured township near Johannesburg. A common platform, known as the Freedom Charter, was adopted. Its principal provisions are:

South Africa belongs to all who live in it, Black and White, and no Government can justly claim authority unless it is based on the will of all the people ...

The rights of the people shall be the same, regardless of race, colour or sex ...

The national wealth of our country, the heritage of all South Africans, shall be restored to the people. The mineral wealth beneath the soil, the banks and monopoly industry, shall be transferred to the ownership of the people as a whole ...

Restriction of land ownership on a racial basis shall be ended, and all the land redivided among those who work it, to banish famine and land hunger.

All shall be equal before the law.

All shall enjoy equal human rights.

There shall be work and security; men and women of all races shall receive equal pay for equal work ...

The doors of learning and culture shall be opened ...

There shall be houses, security and comfort ... peace and friendship.

Chief Luthuli made it clear that, short of violence, there was no instrument of pressure he would not apply on White South Africa to force a change. But he also stated very firmly that he was wholly against any form of racial domination.

I have been told by liberal-minded people (though not members of the Liberal Party) that the image of Congress presented by Chief Luthuli and other leaders is not the true one; that this is in fact a tactical ruse to persuade Whites to accept Congress policies. I reject such suggestions for a number of reasons, not the least being my personal knowledge of many of the leaders. But there are factors which can be objectively assessed. Congress policy is to build up irresistible pressure on White South Africa to force her to abandon racial domination. This aim could plausibly be shown to be most easily and quickly achieved by persistent anti-Whiteism, which could easily be whipped up to a fury. But if anything, Congress has consistently controlled these emotions. It has sharply opposed suggestions of violence. Chief Luthuli and other leaders know that racial emotion might be a short cut to liberation, but in the face of opposition from exponents of the 'tough' line they have defended their multi-racial policies with their political lives.

Communism gained a greater influence on African opinion through the new Congress alliance than it had ever had when the Communist Party functioned legally. This is not to say it had a very great influence; it was simply greater than before. For one thing, the banning of the Communist Party focused African attention on Communism. A party that an oppressive government felt to be so dangerous was made to appear a powerful and valuable ally. A number of African Communists were welcomed into the ranks of the A.N.C. Indian Communists joined the South African Indian Congress, and soon there were two factions in the Indian organization. The old leadership, which stood for negotiation and moderation, was replaced by a far more vigorous, militant and dynamic set of leaders, including a number of Communists. Since an alliance existed with the A.N.C., the Communists were provided with yet another channel of influence. As 'dangerous enemies of the fascist Government', their views were no less welcome than those of the African Communists. When the South African Congress of Democrats and the South African Coloured People's Organization (Congress) joined the alliance, there were yet further channels for Communist persuasion; most members of the all-White Congress of Democrats are Marxists, nearly all of them orthodox Communists. Some of the leading Communists, like Mr Sam Kahn, once a 'natives' representative' in Parliament, stayed out of this body because it was racial and thus opposed to an essential principle of their beliefs — multi-racialism.

Most of the 'named' Communists were soon smelled out by the special police and banned from active work and from holding office in the new organizations. They were not thereby debarred from giving advice secretly — advice made the more welcome by the bannings which, by advertising them as people whom the police thought dangerous, proclaimed them as men and women likely to fight the Nationalists with determination.

The image of Communism in South Africa built up by these people is one of many years of vigorous, determined, sincere and courageous action against racial oppression. Africans themselves have not seen Communism in power, and the fact that unfavourable reports of it come from their oppressors makes these reports seem improbable. Most South African Communists are dedicated to the fight against racial domination, and to the destruction of the racial idea. They have given ex-Chief Luthuli much support in his determined stand against the rise of anti-Whiteism in Congress.

But good and dedicated Communists, like all good and dedicated believers, feel compelled to propagate their creed however and whenever they can. They are not reticent in this; indeed, a number of people in the A.N.C. felt that the Communists were too forward. They claimed that Communism was defacing, if not effacing, African nationalism. They objected to the equal strength of representation of the component groups on the Consultative Committee of the Congress Alliance. Each organization had two representatives. The tiny Congress of Democrats (mainly White Communists) had the same number of delegates as the A.N.C. with its vastly larger membership. The objectors later claimed that elections to the A.N.C.'s controlling councils were rigged against them.

It was these men who, late in 1958, broke away from the African National Congress. Early in 1959 they formed the Pan-Africanist Congress.

It is important to disentangle from the allegations and counter-allegations made at the time what essential differences divided the P.A.C. from the A.N.C. The two streams were present within the

A.N.C. before it split. The A.N.C. believed that while the African people must 'spearhead the struggle against White domination', there was a useful role the other races could play. The Africanists of the P.A.C. believed that Black Africans alone must extricate themselves from the position in which the Whites had put them.

Both movements saw the struggle largely as an economic one in which racial prejudice played an important part. The white man had constructed a system of economic privilege almost wholly aligned with racial differences. To the A.N.C. this meant that all those opposed to the system of racial oppression and its economic results should be united. But the P.A.C. concluded that since all Whites derived some advantage from the system of racial-economic oppression, none of them could be relied on to attack it wholeheartedly.

The Africanists have apparent historical support for their view that White sympathizers have put a brake on drastic Black action against White oppression. The sympathizers have not always consciously set out to do this, but the effect has been the same.

In the nineteen twenties, Joint Councils of Europeans and Africans were founded. They were no more than discussion groups but they attracted a fair number of African intellectuals, many of whom, nurtured as they were in the old Cape tradition, saw themselves as part of a wider community and clung to the hope that they might be accepted as such. By training, their outlook was that of the people of other races with whom they were educated, and they aspired to acceptance among Whites of their own level. Indeed, in 1920 a number of African leaders petitioned Smuts on the colour bar, declaring that it singled out 'our cultured men and women for special treatment, and subjected them to the contempt and insolence of low-grained Whites in all stations, thus directly inciting to mob law and violence'.

The effect of the Joint Councils was to isolate most, though not all, of these African intellectuals from the Native National Congress, and thus deprive it of some of its potential vigour. Certainly White friends of the Cape Africans and of Congress leaders invariably counselled moderation as a means of fostering European 'trust'.

The few Africans in the Cape who voted on the common roll believed that the roll might be expanded, despite the omens of the Act of Union; the few Europeans who really believed that it might were able to convince their African friends that the belief was well founded. Thus African minds were engaged in planning futile political battles when, if they had not been so seduced, they might more quickly have turned to other forms of struggle, and might perhaps have given some virility to the Native Congress. Even in 1936, when the Cape Africans were removed from the common to a separate voters' roll and given their 'own' special White representatives, some African leaders were persuaded by White friends to put their faith in the new system. Most African leaders, however, saw its futility, although some of those White friends later became 'natives' representatives' and fought a good, but hopeless, fight. Clements Kedalie's Industrial and Commercial Workers' Union, which once seemed so strong, cracked after its leader flirted with White sympathizers. He was fêted by trade unionists in Europe, and when he returned from his tour, some of his followers told him that he had 'gone away Black and returned White'.

The integrity of these White sympathizers was almost always beyond reproach. Doubtless they genuinely believed that the course they were following would best serve African interests. But they achieved almost nothing. The Africans, looking back on their work today, conclude that the White liberals handicapped the forging of an effective African unity, postponed the identification of African intellectuals with the ordinary people, and delayed the search for more effective weapons against White domination. They further conclude that if the European sympathizers had left the Africans to forge stronger tools of political struggle out of despair, and to accept the racial challenge to take their rights with their own hands, then subsequent events might never have happened.

This view was not the monopoly of the Africanists; it was shared by many members of the A.N.C. When the Liberal Party appeared in 1953, it seemed to Africans that the earlier pattern would be repeated. The Party advocated a qualified franchise. It was a multi-racial party. It intended to try to attract African members. It proposed no drastic changes in the economic set-up, thus hinting that it might try to divide Africans on the basis of class. With its qualified franchise, it would put in place of the 'race barrier' a 'civilization barrier'. It might again offer hope to numbers of Africans of a parliamentary road to liberation. It might again shake African unity and drain African nationalism of effective leaders.

It was the same with the Communists. They too had weaned a number of African leaders away from the Native National Congress and had sought to supplant Congress as the major liberating movement. During the Second World War, the South African Communists followed the Moscow alignments. When Russia went to war with Hitler, having first fought on his side, they switched their allegiance to Smuts. First they told Africans not to fight in the 'phoney war', then they encouraged them to do so. When the Communist Party was banned and its members flocked to the Congress standard, the Africanists remembered this, and the spectre of the liberal precedent haunted them.

Before very long, in the Africanist view, the Communist allies of Congress became its masters. Africanists alleged that the White Communists and the 'Indian merchant class' controlled Congress, and they charged these people with scrapping the 1949 Programme of Action of the A.N.C. Youth League. They accused them of watering down positive action, because positive action might undermine their own vested interests. They pointed to the motor-cars and attractive houses in the best suburbs owned by many White Communists; they said that the money for these things was earned in a system of White economic privilege. The 'Indian merchant class' had, they said, also acquired assets by 'exploiting' the African masses.

It was in such terms that the new Africanists judged the works of the earlier liberals. They denied these people any sincerity and attacked them as agents of White domination, sent to divide and rule. Today, the Africanists speak of 'such movements of the ruling class as Moral Rearmament, the Congress of Democrats and the Liberal Party'. To almost all Africans, to the whole of the Congress of Democrats and to most Liberals, Moral Rearmament seems, indeed, to be an organization designed to blunt the militancy of African opposition. (It is seen in this way because it tells Africans to 'change themselves' and wait for the Whites to 'change themselves'.) However, it is misleading and emotional to identify this movement with the Congress of Democrats and the Liberal Party.

Most Liberals, Communists and loyal members of the A.N.C. said at first that the Africanists were merely cloaking their anti-White sentiments with implausible pseudo-economic arguments. Certainly this was my own first reaction. Many people understood only too well the Africanists' reluctance to work with Whites in the light of the past effects of such co-operation, but they felt that the understandable reluctance had turned into a racialistic outlook.

The Africanists claimed that the A.N.C. acceptance of the Freedom Charter was a deviation from the original objectives of the Native National Congress. The Charter, they said, spoke of 'the people of South Africa, Black and White together', while the P.A.C., like the old Native Congress, spoke 'of and for the African people'[1] whom 'it regards as part of one African nation'. Their case has been stated by Mr P. N. Raboroko, the Secretary for Education and a member of the P.A.C. National Executive Committee:

> Nationalism demands that the interests of indigenous peoples should dominate over those of aliens because the country belongs to the indigenous peoples. Socialism demands that the interests of the workers should dominate over those of their employers because their contribution to the creation

[1] The Native National Congress had used the words 'Native people'.

of wealth is more significant than that of their bosses. Democracy demands that those of the majority should dominate over those of the minority because they are a majority. In Africa in general and in South Africa in particular, the African people are indigenous to the soil, are the real workers, and are the majority. Their right to the effective control of their own interests is therefore unchallengeable.

The gravamen of the Africanist charge against the Charterists [the A.N.C.] therefore is that they have betrayed the material interests of the African people. They have sacrificed these interests upon the political altar of an ungodly alliance, an alliance of slave-owner, slave-driver and slave...

'And therefore we, the people of South Africa,' proclaims the ultimate clause [of the Freedom Charter], 'Black and White together — equals, countrymen and brothers — adopt this Freedom Charter ... '

To them master and slave — the exploiter and the exploited, the oppressor and the oppressed, the degrader and the degraded — are all equals. To them indigenous African nationals and immigrant European foreign nations — the dispossessed and their dispossessors, the victims and their robbers — are all countrymen. For them the progressive and the reactionary — the African subject and his foreign overlord, the African nationalist and the colonialist or white supremacist, the liberationist and the collaborationist — are all brothers.

The problem of the synthesis of opposites cannot be resolved by the wave of the magic wand. It is only after all these sets of antithetical categories have been duly reconciled that we can reach those final categories — equals, countrymen and brothers — which betray no instability. Such ultimate reconciliation is possible only in Africanism, the final synthesis of these categories which the Africanist manifesto defines as 'the social force which upholds the material and spiritual interests of the individual'.[1]

It was obviously never the intention of the Freedom Charter to 'reconcile' White and Black while maintaining White economic privilege. On the contrary, Congress moved towards a socialist policy in adopting the Charter. The Africanist thesis that no white man can act other than in self-interest does seem anti-White in spirit. The Africanists were, however, convinced that they had enough evidence to justify it. They were sure that the most powerful weapon for Africans was the discipline of the strong sentiment of African nationalism, tinged, if necessary, with the dynamic force of racialism. This discipline would carry the African masses into concerted campaigns, and into the Programme of Positive Action. Could Africans get the same kind of inspiration from the A.N.C.'s non-racial ideal? In co-operation with Whites whose very 'brothers' oppressed Blacks? The Africanists felt that the alliance led to a blurring of colour consciousness. And colour consciousness was fundamental to the African struggle in the racial strait-jacket of South Africa.

Was it possible to stimulate mass action against a system of White oppression while restraining feelings of malice towards individual white men? Was not resentment of Whites as a group a most natural reaction to White domination? If anti-White feeling added to the militancy of African resistance and promised to bring African liberation nearer, was it to be deplored? The Africanists asked the A.N.C. why they were more concerned to reassure Whites against Black domination than to achieve a speedier liberation of Africans.

The effect of this kind of thinking is well illustrated by the experience of a prominent White liberal, a teacher in an African school, who set his pupils to writing an essay on 'What I would do if the Africans gained power'. The best essay was written by a boy

[1] P. N. Raboroko: 'The Africanist Case'. *Africa South*, Vol. 4, No. 3, April-June 1960.

who promised to cut the throats of all the white men. The teacher, as usual, asked the author to read his work to the class and answer questions afterwards. The teacher's own question to the boy was whether he would also cut his schoolmaster's throat. The boy replied: 'Yes, sir. I would cut your throat first, because you are the people who prevent my people from seeing how bad your people really are.'

* * *

The African National Congress did not take the Africanist charges against it lying down. It vigorously denied rigging elections and asserted that it was not under White control. The P.A.C. boasted that its membership would be one hundred thousand by July 31st, 1959, but by April 1960 it could claim only thirty thousand. In January 1960, the A.N.C. said that P.A.C. membership was, in fact, only two thousand five hundred. The A.N.C. charged that the small membership of the P.A.C. was a reflection of the limited support for its principles which there had been inside the Congress, a support too small to be a threat to the leadership of the A.N.C. (There are no published figures for A.N.C. membership, but its leaders estimate this at between a hundred and fifty thousand and two hundred thousand.)

The African National Congress pointed to its crowded meetings as a demonstration of continued mass support after the breakaway. It was the shootings at Sharpeville and Langa that rocketed the P.A.C. into prominence throughout the world. Three African National Congress leaders have told me that the crowds that gathered at Sharpeville were not members or supporters of the P.A.C. According to these accounts, there was a hard core of Africanists; a larger number were 'enticed' to the police-station on various pretexts — one of which was a story allegedly put about that the police were to make an important announcement regarding passes; still more people, the story goes, were rounded up by Africanist agents from the early morning bus queues, and the rest went out of curiosity. The Bishop of Johannesburg, the Right Reverend Ambrose Reeves, has stated this point of view in his *Shooting at Sharpeville*.

The Africanists claim that the crowds were orderly, peaceful and passive; there to protest against the passes. The A.N.C men who gave me their view cited the passivity as proof that the crowds were not fully aware of what was going on. They did not, it is said, realize that they were there as part of the P.A.C. protest. The police tried to excuse the massacre of so many people by alleging that the crowds were dangerous, hostile and threatening, which would suggest that they were actively protesting. But the police account was not supported by the abundance of evidence given by independent eye-witnesses. Moreover, the Government has said that it will introduce legislation indemnifying itself against claims by people who lost breadwinners in the shootings, thus strengthening the inference that the police were culpable.

It can be safely assumed, from this and from the reports of the judicial commissions, that the crowd was passive. That alone, however, is not positive proof either of the A.N.C. claim that the crowd gathered in ignorance of the purpose of the meeting, or of the P.A.C. claim that they were all there to protest, in an orderly fashion, against the passes.

The A.N.C. claims that the African people hold the police and the P.A.C. jointly responsible for the Sharpeville martyrdoms: the police for the actual killings, the P.A.C. for its 'untimely' and 'irresponsible' action. The A.N.C. was about to organize its own anti-pass protests, which, my informants claimed, were better planned. The P.A.C. tried to jump the gun and acted without assessing the consequences.

The P.A.C. leaders in Sharpeville, I was told, 'dare not poke their noses into the township' and fled to Basutoland, not so much in fear of the police as in fear of the 'vengeance of the African people'. The implication is that the prestige and influence of the P.A.C. are now at a lower ebb than they were before Sharpeville, and that the size of the Sharpeville crowds was no indication of P.A.C. membership or support.

The A.N.C. officially accuses the P.A.C. of racialism. The P.A.C. it says, does not so much attack the Socialists, Marxists and Communists in the A.N.C. as the Congress alliance with Whites who happen to be Socialists, Marxists or Communists. The P.A.C. speaks of the 'White pseudo-leftist directorate of the A.N.C.' The Secretary-General of the A.N.C., Mr Duma Nokwe, spoke in reply of the 'poisonous and sterile racialism that they [the P.A.C.] often expound. For this, of course, the bludgeons of White supremacy are alone to blame. The intransigence of apartheid must inevitably lead to a Black intransigence equally demented.'

The A.N.C. was proud that the accused in the Treason Trial were drawn from all the different racial groups in South Africa. It says this is proof of the dedication to African liberation of the White, Indian and Coloured allies of Congress. These allies have put themselves in great personal danger. The A.N.C. officially repudiates the charge that it has in any way abandoned the 1949 Programme of Action or that White concern for vested interests has been exercised to water down positive action. The programme, says the A.N.C., was carried out, and it was precisely because this was so that there was a treason trial in which Whites were among the accused.

Any kind of anti-Whiteism, the A.N.C. felt, would lead to frustrated and spontaneous outbursts of violence which the White supremacists would suppress ruthlessly, relishing the act. The A.N.C. claimed it had learnt, though the P.A.C. had not, that the Whites had secret police to detect any incipient violent resistance, and the men and materials to crush it. Even at Sharpeville, the claim goes on, the nervous Whites had only begun to flex their muscles. All that Sharpeville achieved was the banning of both Congresses. I might add that this does not mean that either is dead; on the contrary, the Congress itself has gone underground and the P.A.C. can be expected to do the same. Both will, of course, propagate their respective philosophies undergound, but the bannings can only hinder their work by removing their leaders.

For some time after the Sharpeville and Langa shootings, African opposition seemed to be punch drunk, and no doubt the example that the police had made of the Sharpeville and Langa demonstrators, the subsequent state of emergency, and the imprisonment of and restrictions on leaders, were part of the reason for the apparent lull in African activity.

Late in 1960, however, it was the activists of the former A.N.C. who came back strongly inside South Africa. (Abroad, men of both the banned African movements were working together in a South Africa United Front.) The former A.N.C. activists were busy convening an All-African Conference, which would try to create some unity among the personnel of the two main organizations.

The conference was held in Johannesburg and was attended by prominent Africans, not only from the former A.N.C. and P.A.C., but also from the Liberal Party and a large number of non-political organizations. A continuation committee was established which included leading members of the Liberal Party. Quite soon, there were 'disclosures' of Communist manipulation of the conference — and all the old charges of White control and masterminding. The Pan-Africanists withdrew, and with them two leading African Liberals from Natal. Transvaal African Liberals remained, however.

The Continuation Committee then convened an All-African Delegates Conference in Pietermaritzburg, representing one hundred and forty-five African organizations, but not before all the members and ex-members of the Committee had been arrested. Enemies of the organizers alleged that the real delegates were swamped by a large number of persons purporting to be representatives, but specially imported from Durban to flood the Conference.

Mr Nelson Mandela, who had been under restriction and was a former member of the executive of the banned A.N.C., made the keynote speech at the conference and afterwards described its

AFRICANS AND AFRICANISTS

theme as 'African unity, and the calling by the Government of a national convention of elected representatives of all adult men and women on an equal basis, irrespective of race, colour or creed, with powers to determine a new democratic constitution for South Africa'. The conference resolved that if the Government failed to call this convention by May 31st [1961], countrywide demonstrations would be held on the eve of the Republic in protest against this undemocratic act ... All sections of the African population would be asked to unite in opposing the Nationalists.

A National Action Council was elected to implement the decisions of the Conference, and Mr Mandela formulated the demands made in a letter to the Prime Minister. Needless to say, the Government refused to act, and the mass demonstrations were planned to coincide with the Republican declaration. A general strike was to be staged.

South Africa's exit from the Commonwealth and the strong resolution passed by the U.N. at its April 1961 session lifted the morale of the victims of apartheid enormously and made it possible that the call for action might meet with a considerable response. This prompted the biggest police raids on African townships and White liberal homes that the country had ever seen; the search was on for documents and leaflets announcing the strike and other demonstrations. The Government rushed through legislation empowering the Attorney-General to detain any person for twelve days before bringing a charge in the courts, and so remove all key persons from the scene. It was clear, even then, that whatever the outcome of the strike proposals, the A.N.C. activists again held the centre of the stage. The P.A.C., it is said, called on the African people to disobey the strike call. The outcome itself is now a part of history, and the only firm conclusion is that it confirms the increasing brutality of the South African Government. (The three-day strike was held to be successful only in Johannesburg, for one day.) What remains uncertain is whether the A.N.C. has ousted the P.A.C., or is itself in danger of displacement.

169

The accusations of Communist manipulation remain, and they now come not only from the P.A.C. but from some Liberals also. Some African Liberals holding key posts in the National Action Council claim that decisions were made and action taken without their knowledge; that they were put into key positions to create a façade behind which a small clique was operating. The May 31st demonstrations have not brought about the downfall of the Government, and those opposed to the methods of the A.N.C. activists—the P.A.C. men—may well renew their call for Africans to go it alone on the grounds that 'White-controlled' demonstrations are doomed to failure. Limited successes may have been achieved, but the only objective which really matters remains the downfall of the Government.

* * *

Africanism and demented Afrikaner nationalism are not dissimilar, even though there are vast differences between them. Certain trends and events in Afrikaner history are being repeated by the Africanists, but it is not these similarities which are of real importance. Both African and Afrikaner would, I realize, feel insulted by comparisons of the inward forces that drive them; both see their reactions not as reactions, but as a positive part of their natural selves.

The Afrikaner nationalist's view of Africans as inferiors is the view formed by his ancestors when they first met black people centuries ago. This view has become a part of Afrikanerdom and an essential part of its nationalism. But the Afrikaner has in turn suffered from a deep sense of inferiority in his dealings with the British. The arrogant British view of Afrikaners as inferior has so affected them that they have been mercilessly driven to prove themselves, not only to the rest of the world, but to themselves.

In Afrikaner nationalism there is an ingredient which has for centuries dominated its thinking. The ingredient is fear. It is impossible to isolate this fear from Afrikaner nationalism or to discuss it rationally with Afrikaners, because they have come to submerge it in their *Weltanschauung*. Fear, however, is not a part either of African nationalism or of Africanism, though racial bitterness may be; and the absence of fear may mean that Africanism will soon exhaust itself.

If the Africanists could understand that some of the things they do and say mirror the Nationalist Government, they might be able to accept that certain of their reactions are legitimate, but that others should be curbed. For instance, it is Government policy to forbid mixing of White and Black and to prevent Whites from entering African townships. Anti-Whiteism would make both impossible even without laws against them.

Like Afrikaners vis-à-vis the English in the past, Africanists feel a need to counter the widespread White belief in African inferiority. Later, we see the effect of it on Africanists themselves. How do they smash the belief among Whites who would never otherwise be reconciled to majority rule? Most Whites insist that Africans cannot organize themselves and look for the White masterminds of their successes. Only by clearly rejecting White help can Africanists explode the myth.

There are at present a number of fundamental features in the Africanist programme which, unless abandoned, will keep the Africans at arm's length from any White sympathizer, however much the white man tries to get closer, *and however much he contributes to African liberation*. P.A.C. spokesmen have been quite uncompromising in their repudiation of the suggestion that their attitudes are a reaction to their treatment at the hands of Whites. They say that the South African Native National Congress was established as a nationalist organization in 1912, before Hertzog came to power and thirty-six years before Malan formed his Government. Their objectives, they claim, are the same now as then, and the events of intervening years have not influenced them in any way. African nationalism, they say, was an inevitable force that would have arisen even if there had been no White domination.

This is hardly borne out by the facts. Some of the objectives of 1912 may, on paper, be the same as those of the Africanists, but there are vast differences. Indeed, the Native Congress was brought into being in reaction to the Act of Union. The Africanists not only reject the idea that Whites could have any positive influence on them; they go further and are repelled by the idea that Whites can influence them even negatively; that anything they do is a reaction (conscious or unconscious) to anything Whites do to them.

The Africanists need to prove themselves to themselves to answer White slanders, because they have to a certain extent been affected themselves by the constant clap-trap talked about racial inferiority. Quite naturally, they do not recognize the reason for this need to prove themselves, nor do they concede the point. The driving force exists inside them, and the attitude is submerged in their wider belief in Africanism. The motivation of it is not grasped. It has attached itself to African nationalism in other parts of the continent, but nowhere is it such a strong force as in the Union. 'I would be disappointed,' Mr Sobukwe, leader of the P.A.C., said to me once, 'if the Africans were to get their rights without having to work and struggle for them.' To the P.A.C., this urge for positive assertion has become an objective in itself, an inseparable part of the goal of liberation. In other words, as they see it, liberation without assertion is not liberation. Their concept of liberation differs from that of those who see it merely as the economic and political emancipation of the African people.

Africanism has given to its exponents — and its victims — a view of life as *oppressed Africans*. Precisely because they are oppressed Africans, they feel that no one else can be a part of their society, nor can anyone else participate in *their* struggle. Because certain attitudes have become bound up with African nationalism, they are regarded as integral parts of it.

In so far as African nationalism throughout the continent is 'a struggle against White supremacy', no one can justly fault it. If the Africanist rejection of co-operation with Whites were motivated solely (or even primarily) by the urge for the *speediest* political and economic emancipation of the Africans, then whether or not one accepted that it was indeed the speediest course, it would be hard to blame the Africanists. It is this blank refusal to work openly with Whites that leads to the charge of anti-Whiteism against Africanists.

Nothing could be more natural than anti-Whiteism in South Africa. My own first reaction to Africanist policy was to attack it because I instinctively saw it as anti-White. I later came to realize, however, that White liberals who did this would only be adding fuel to the flame. After a little further thought, I felt that liberals should look at themselves very closely before attacking Africanists as completely anti-White. Superficially they might seem anti-White; but on closer examination it might be that there was something in what they had to say. Perhaps the White liberal conviction that their policies were completely non-racial was faulty in some way; perhaps by some omission in their policies they failed to accord the Africanists some legitimate right.

Trying to understand the P.A.C. does not mean that the White liberals must repudiate the A.N.C., or in any way be less co-operative with them. On the contrary, they should try to reunify the two groups. They were divided over the question of co-operation with Whites; to that extent, such Whites are obstacles to re-unification. The only beneficiaries of division are the Nationalist oppressors. A speedy liberation of Africans requires early unity. If the Whites allied to Congress could, after some self-examination, discover what it was that the Africanists objected to, if there is any justice in the Africanist argument, and if the White allies could go some way to meet Africanist grievances, then, perhaps, they could facilitate a reconciliation. It may not be possible, but they should try it.

Racialism may not be the sole cause of the Africanist refusal to accept White support. There is no doubt that there have in the past been some unfortunate results of White co-operation with Africans. White liberals should therefore ask themselves: 'What was *our* basic objective? Was it to deliver Africans from White domination as soon as possible? Or were we more concerned, through our aim of a common society, to ensure that White domination would not simply be replaced by Black supremacy?' The two objectives could be very different.

The Liberal Party, as one element of the White liberals, once took the line that it stood in the 'middle of the road' between White nationalism and Black nationalism. As the party's Transvaal Organizing Secretary, I wrote in the Johannesburg *Star* in February 1959:

> If we have anything to fear for the future in South Africa, it is exclusive and sectional Black nationalism — and not a common society ... There are two trends in African politics: the one is towards exclusive nationalism, and the other is towards a broad South African patriotism in which race-pride and arrogance can be eliminated.
>
> The trouble is that both of these are anathema to South African Whites, and they resist both with an equal vigour. The more they resist the idea of a common society, the more do they strengthen the hands of the extremists, simply because extremism sets up a reaction of extremism.
>
> The Liberal Party's objective for the future is therefore a common society ... It must seek to strengthen the hands of the non-White moderates ... The Party's growth as a Parliamentary group is but one means of achieving its important objective.

Anxious to find out more about their policies, I met some of the Africanists privately. It was clear that they had read what I had written and resented it. This prompted a little introspection on my part. The result was that I saw the possibility that the quickest way to liberation might be along the road of exclusive Black nationalism, even embittered Black nationalism, if necessary. What else, after all, would drive Africans to throw themselves in their thousands against the fortress of White domination—so over-whelming that they could not all be stopped by force, so numerous that they could not all be arrested, so determined that they carried on till the very end? Was I certain that I knew of a quicker way? And if I was not certain, was I aware that my own presence was blurring the colour awareness that would give the Africanists their driving force?

In a subsequent article I tried to show that it was possible that the attainment of a common society could, in fact, bring African liberation. I could not say definitely that it could do so more quickly than exclusive African nationalism, but it was important, I thought, to show that the Liberal Party, at any rate, did not place one objective above the other.

A young Africanist, with whom I was friendly, bitterly attacked this second article when he and I were together with a group of Africans in a township the following Sunday. I had, he said, called for the 'reconciliation of master and servant'. I was distressed, but I realized, much later, how he could have come to this interpre-tation of what I had said. He had seen more clearly than I that his disabilities, although the result of prejudice against the colour of his skin, also had underlying economic causes. Because I had failed to deal with the economic aspects of the colour bar I had, to his mind, *perhaps deliberately* ignored the disproportion of the White and the non-White share in the national economy. It had therefore seemed that I wanted the black man, via non-racialism, to accept a changed political situation, while possibly wanting to maintain economic privilege. The White feared not only Black domination; he also wished to remain economically on top. If the policy that I was proposing could satisfy him and allay his fears, it could only mean that I was not proposing any basic alteration of the economy. The incident taught me not only how omission could set minds wondering, but also how dangerous it was im-mediately to answer attack with counter-attack.

I had, of course, also failed to realize that African group asser-tion had become an end in itself; if Africanists did not themselves bring about their own liberation they would for ever be tortured with the need to assert the African personality, to 'prove themselves' and disprove the White myth that the black man is inferior.

At this time I met in Johannesburg a young American, Allard Lowenstein, who was a former president of the American students' union and a foreign affairs adviser to Senator Hubert Humphrey. He had established excellent relations with African leaders in both the A.N.C. and the P.A.C. In his discussions with P.A.C. leaders, I had been quoted as a 'white man with whom it was impossible to work'. Allard, I was later informed, defended me. As a result of talks with him, I eventually spent some profitable hours with Mr Robert Sobukwe, leader of the P.A.C.

During our conversations I began to realize what it was in my own thinking that the Africanists could *legitimately and justly criticize*. When I left Mr Sobukwe, I felt that there was room for a movement like the Liberal Party to alter its programme, thereby removing intended acts and omissions which could legitimately be criticized. But I also felt that there was an unbridgeable gap between the Africanists and *any White* sympathizer. This gap was the difference in the colour of their skins. It was the Africanist consciousness of this difference which created the gap and kept it open.

If it is accepted that the goal of liberation might be most speedily reached by unleashing the mighty force of bitterness against the white man, then, at least for some of the Africanists, the means will become an end in itself. The passion that was intended as the vehicle of liberation will become obsessive. Certainly the neurotic anti-White racialist on the African side will find ample emotional outlet in the movement. And why should anyone in it bother to check him?

It is in this respect that the Pan-Africanists in South Africa differ from those elsewhere in Africa. In Ghana, for instance, Dr Nkrumah has assiduously set his face against anti-Whiteism as a structural feature of this political philosophy.

It is, of course, of great importance for Liberals on their side to reduce the differences that divide them from the Pan-Africanists, even though these Africans preserve an impassable barrier. Some — though not all — the aspects of the Liberal policies which the Africanists criticize, are also objectionable to the A.N.C., so that in moving closer to the P.A.C., Liberals might also settle outstanding differences with the A.N.C. The Liberal Party has only partially grasped the differences between itself and the A.N.C., because it is a coalition of people with different views on economics, wholly agreed only on the evils of racialism.

It is difficult to attempt a forecast of what is likely to be the dominant African mood of the future. Will it be the spirit of racial co-operation that the A.N.C. officially espouses, or will it be the attitude of the P.A.C.? We can be quite certain that there will be a great deal of anti-Whiteism; even A.N.C. members sometimes confess to it. The White man could, after all, hardly have behaved worse. But the question is whether anti-Whiteism will dominate the mood of Africans.

Anti-Whiteism can, of course, be averted if solutions like those I suggest later in this book can be applied in time. But that may be too much to hope for.

Until recently, the aspiration of most Africans, like that of American Negroes, has been to integrate properly into the existing society, changing it substantially, perhaps, but by and large keeping the present structure. Thus, African power would be used to maintain the basic values and standards as they exist at present. By and large, that was the view of the A.N.C., in spite of their desire for a wider continental unity.

The P.A.C. aim, however, represents a growing feeling that Africans should fashion a new society, leaving the Europeans to fit in as best they can. The end-product that the Africanist sees is something like the Ghanaian pattern.

South Africa has an urban proletariat three million strong, a great part of which has been urbanized for decades. The ambitions of individual people in the cities have been shaped in a very different mould from that of most other African countries; not only are the wants of Africans greater (because more of them have seen more things to want), but education and detribalization have been more extensive and intensive than anywhere else in Africa. Though these factors apply less strongly to the rural Africans of South Africa, they still apply more strongly than to Africans in other places, so that the aspirations of even the rural Africans have been formulated in a different context.

There are those who believe that these facts alone make it inevitable that Africans will want to integrate into the existing society rather than fashion a new one. According to this thesis, the industrial proletariat of South Africa has widely divergent objectives from those of the very different and less developed urban masses of say, Ghana. Communists in the Union argue that the aims of this proletariat will be no different from those of highly industrialized peoples anywhere else in the world. This point of view overlooks the other influences at work among Africans. Some people even argue that the African has not revolted against the *status quo* because the highly developed economy gives him a higher living standard level than Africans have elsewhere. (The real reason for the continued existence of the *status quo* is that it has been so difficult to overthrow.)

The P.A.C. and A.N.C. are now engaged in an underground struggle for the allegiance of Africans, and already the A.N.C. has been reminded that it must keep its sights on Pan-African unity. It is probably the P.A.C. rather than the A.N.C. which will become stronger, the longer White domination persists. For one thing, anti-Whiteism will become more obsessive.

The Africanist belief in their policy as a unifying and liberating force will gather strength if the policies of racial co-operation show themselves apparently incapable of defeating White domination. Emotion will then supplant logic. Far from believing that their material well-being depends on preserving the highly-developed White-controlled economy, many Africans may then be led into thinking, like the Congolese, that a far easier path to well-being lies in simply expropriating ill-gotten White gains. The economy would go to rack and ruin, but the lesson could only be learned from bitter experience; no amount of warning could avert it. Another factor would then come into operation: the assertion of the African's personality and the urge to prove himself capable of doing things as well as his former White masters.

The only existing safeguard for the future is that now operating in, say, Ghana. The political consciousness of the African masses was awakened by their own huge role in the liberation of their country. If the promises of widespread improvement of individual standards are not fulfilled, this mass awakening is channelled into new demands for social reform. A crippled economy cannot guarantee these improvements, and African technical deficences will demand the importation of technicians, entrepreneurs, capital and experts, if those on the spot have been expelled or killed during the course of liberation.

Many South Africans claim that the P.A.C. has lost ground by going back on some of its policies. Before Sharpeville, the leaders said that, when breaking the pass laws, they would accept no bail, pay no fines, accept no defence and make no appeal in any subsequent trial and conviction. Some of the leaders appealed, however, and fines have been paid for others. Nevertheless, I am quite sure, that Sobukwe and his associates will emerge from prison with greatly enhanced prestige.

It is my belief that an African Sinn Fein ('We Ourselves') will make advances in South Africa, if not through the P.A.C. itself, then through some other movement. Its exponents may then persuade Pan-Africanists elsewhere in Africa that anti-Whiteism is the quickest way to liberation in the south. Continental Pan-Africanism — now a non-racialist force — might then no longer be a guarantee against the rise of anti-Whiteism in South Africa — at least in the immediate future.

The challenge that faces liberals in this situation faces every white man in Africa. It does more. It faces the Western world in its relations with Africa.

GUILTY LAND

If the liberals could find a meeting-point with both the A.N.C. and the P.A.C., it would provide a supreme example for the West in its dealings with Africa. In that sense, this book is addressed, not to the Liberal Party, nor even to the Afrikaner, but to white men everywhere.

Whatever other factors dictate the course that liberals should follow, they should be guided very clearly by a desire for a closer understanding between the A.N.C. and the P.A.C. If liberals attack the Africanist spirit, it may well set the seal on the future course of their policies. Liberals do not act in a vacuum, but in a situation in which there are already a million stimuli of anti-White sentiment. The better course, at this juncture, is to intensify their efforts to end the oppression of the Africans by Whites, and to bring about those changes in themselves which can help to bridge — from the liberal side — the gap dividing liberals from Africanists.

The Pan-Africanist Congress insists that its objective in South Africa is 'non-racialism'. Its doors will be open to Whites when — and only when — it has smashed the White concept of Africans as inferior, and after it has attained African liberation. Whether it is possible to work towards non-racialism with the methods used by the P.A.C. is very much an open question.

CHAPTER III

THE ROLE OF THE LIBERALS

THE first aim of liberals in Africa must be the liberation of the African people. By liberation I mean complete political and economical emancipation. They must not try to create a tactical political image which would cloak some other aim. It must be an end in itself, striven for directly, passionately — *and regardless of the consequences*. They must not falter even if it becomes obvious that liberation will release a flood of embittered African nationalism, for the Africanists will not, of course, be content with the White liberal concept of liberation, and will use their new economic and political freedom to move towards their own goal. That prospect must not deter White liberals in any way.

The priority which they give to their objectives will be reflected in their actions; if they put a brake on any action that they know would hasten African liberation, they will, by virtue of that, be judged to have subordinated liberation to some other aim. They must never hamper or obstruct any measure that would more quickly achieve the prime goal. Let us examine the implication of this mood.

In South Africa, liberals, whether in or outside the party of that name, are non-racialists, by definition, who aim at non-racialism. If there are signs of anti-Whiteism — of racialism — among those for whose liberation they work, the time to fight it will come. Then, but only then, they can be as drastic in their choice of weapons as they are now in their fight against White racialism, and that time will come if Black racialists echo the White racialists of today. The liberals and non-racialists will have little real room for complaint, however, if the position of the Whites under Black rule is no worse than that of Blacks in the American South or in other White countries. The most that South African Whites can hope for in such circumstances is that Black anti-racialists in Central and Northern Africa will go as far in protecting White rights in the African South, as White anti-racialists in the American North go —and have gone — in protecting Black rights in the American South. It would be really tragic if Indians and Coloureds were to be the victims of an exclusive Black racialism in the future, because so many of them have suffered under White domination. But they will be much better advocates of their own cause — and indeed of non-racialism — than any white man could be, precisely because they did suffer. As people of colour they would be in a key position to invoke the assistance of the Asian world against any possible infringement of their fundamental human rights.

What the liberals must seek is the *quickest* road to liberation. Is it the path of extreme Black nationalism in the Union? That is certainly one road, and there is no doubt that it would once have been the fastest; it is questionable whether it is now. A combination of external and internal action might seem to be a speedier route, and I hope to show in the next chapter that this would best be helped by non-racial co-operation under African leadership rather than by exclusive Africanism.

The lesson for the Western world is just as clear. Africans must be given their political and economic freedom because it is right, proper and just for them to have it. It must be given regardless of the consequences. Aid must be given to Africa, and given till it hurts. It must be given because it is needed, given on African terms, and given so that Africans may learn to develop their own economies. The Western world, which has taken so much out of Africa, owes her a debt of honour. The debt must be paid. Aid must be given, not because it might buy allies, not because it is enlightened self-interest to give; not in competition with Russia, but because it is Africa's due.

THE ROLE OF THE LIBERALS

Britain, for example, must repay the Africans not only in her own colonies, but in South Africa, which an earlier generation handed to the Boers on a silver platter. I think that this debt only be repaid by a strong British initiative on the South African question in the United Nations.

The West must treat the people of African origin in their midst as they treat themselves, for no other reason than that it is right and just to do so.

The West, quite as much as liberals in Africa, must recognize that the spirit of continental Pan-Africanism is very powerful indeed. So is the urge for African unity. This force is bound to grow in Kenya and Tanganyika, in the Congo, the Rhodesias, and throughout West Africa. It will grow despite — perhaps because of — men like the rulers of Katanga. Only a wider unity can give to Africans a sense of security and the feeling of being their own masters in the face of their tremendous economic and technical dependence on others.

The spirit of men such as Nkrumah will survive that of men apparently more amenable to the West, and indeed, if the West seeks to play the moderates off against the so-called extremists, it will find real extremism supplanting even the mood of Kwame Nkrumah. If he and the men who think like him seem uncompromising, it is only because they stand more strongly for the primacy of African interests than the men who are now called moderates. Sooner or later the Western world must come to terms with these so-called extremists. Sooner is better than later. Later may be too late.

If the White liberals in Africa make non-racialism their prime objective, if they set this above the aim of African liberation, the priority will be reflected in their actions. Africans will say that the liberal object is 'not to give us our liberation; they can see that with liberation spreading in the continent, with the changing attitude of the world, our own liberation is closer; they come now with their doctrine of non-racialism, not so much to change the

183

white man, but to save him from us. Non-racialism is a policy to
safeguard the position of Whites.'

The difficulties that face liberals as components of a wider opposition front are many. If there were signs that the P.A.C., for
example, had racialist tendencies, liberals would still be bound to
act with extreme circumspection before they so arraigned them.
The Africanists are not *now* in power; they are not *now* curtailing
human rights; indeed, they are upholding these rights, by word
and deed. Of course they *might* unleash emotions that would at
some future date make the maintenance of civil liberty difficult,
but they do not set out with this in mind. They set out primarily
to liberate their people by the quickest possible means, and the
suspension of civil liberties may be a consequence of their methods.
They are not the makers of the anti-White sentiment that would
provide the disciplinary force for their resistance movement. The
Liberal Party, for example, sees itself as the custodian of the fundamental freedoms; the Africans and the Africanists are the
aggrieved people. Both Africanists and Liberals seek the removal
of the grievances; the Liberals because they object to the curtailment of human rights, the Africanists because they object to the
curtailment of the rights of Africans. They seek not only the positive assertion of the African personality; they go beyond the demand for African control; they insist on *Africanist* control. If
Liberals (and liberals) are to win African support for their cause,
it will be by showing how hard they will fight for it; what sacrifices
they will make on its behalf against those who are now assailing
it — the White supremacists. This is not the time for sermonizing
about human rights in the future to people who do not have them
today, and least of all about the human rights of the very people
who now deny them theirs.

The time may now be ripe to attack any signs of racialism found
in independent African states, but only where it is absolutely certain that it *is* racialism by Liberal standards. Now is not the time
to do so in subject African states. And even in the free African
states, Liberals must ask themselves before they criticize: what

about Afro-Americans in the southern states of America and coloured people in Britain?

Although the Liberal Party of South Africa has gone a long way to show that its prime aim is the liberation of the African people, it still has a long road to travel. If it had kept to 'parliamentary and constitutional' action and the attempt to persuade White voters to change their views, it would have been tailoring its policies — rather like the Progressives do now — to the White voter's view of the situation. Their hope of parliamentary and electoral change would have been kept alive, holding in check any shift towards the African viewpoint. But the hope is an illusory one, because even if the Party made some gains among English-speaking people, it could never win Nationalist votes without advocating the reinstitution of slavery. Consequently, the Party is now closer to the African viewpoint. Indeed, it encourages action calculated to bring about a speedier liberation and has participated in it, but this — as we have seen — may have its own pitfalls if Liberals cross African nationalists in any way.

Liberals believe that there must be universal suffrage in South Africa because it is just. White South Africa does not generally oppose the principle of universal suffrage: indeed, the Afrikaners have given the vote to all Whites over the age of eighteen. But all Blacks are excluded. Those who call for a qualified franchise do so in the name of good government, but no one can pretend that the call is anything more than a pretext for racial discrimination. The real fear in the minds of these people is that African chauvinism might one day do to the Whites what the Whites now do to Africans. A qualified franchise is a device for postponing this feared situation. But democracy, like justice, must not only be done; it must be seen to be done. How is the African, barred from voting because he lacks certain qualifications, to be convinced that he has not been excluded on the grounds of his colour alone? Even if the qualifications apply to Whites as well, he is still unconvinced because most barriers include educational qualifications, and there is compulsory education for Whites but not for Africans. We are speaking, after all, of a country where the white man has constantly whittled down the civil rights of the black man; the White exponents of non-racialism have a barrier of suspicion to break through. They will discredit their philosophy if there is a suspicion of bias in its application. The longer Whites postpone the extension of the franchise, the more will Black bitterness grow. There will not be less bitterness in South Africa in ten years time, but more. The 'danger of Black domination' will be greater.

The advocates of a qualified franchise are afraid that South Africa has passed the point of no return. Afrikaner nationalism and White domination have sown their seeds of hatred which, they say, have already taken root. I cannot believe that it would be an act of justice to protect the Whites from the consequences of their own actions by further restricting the African's right to vote. A people denied the vote must express their common will in some other way — through strikes, passive resistance, boycott, riot or revolution. Is it not better to train people from the start to express themselves by means of the ballot?

What a people aspires to will be shaped by their background, their level of education, the way the world treats them. Their aspirations will exist, whether or not they have the vote. Admittedly, less developed people may be more gullible in believing the promises of vote-seeking politicians, but the same politicians can use the same slogans to incite the same gullible people to violence. They need only exploit the widespread grievances which exist regardless of whether or not the Black people are denied the franchise. Black chauvinism will be the result of the postponed extension of franchise, rather than of the extension itself.

In South Africa there are more non-White graduates than in any other territory in Africa; education is more widespread, thanks to the missionaries, and there is a more widespread political consciousness. Economic and political sights are set higher because the African in the Union has a better view of higher standards than he has anywhere else. As the result of a harder struggle, he has a more realistic attitude towards hard work. Many Africans in South Africa have appreciated that the Whites possess technological knowledge, business knowledge and a high degree of initiative which has resulted in an expansion of the economy unparalleled elsewhere on the continent. I believe that if the Whites came to their senses, even at this late stage, the Africans would not want to expel them, but to share their knowledge and allow all to profit fairly from their mutual contributions to the country. But it would be foolish to say that this will always be the case.

Liberals both in and outside the Liberal Party have learned that it is not persuasion of White voters or fancy franchise proposals that will alter the situation in South Africa, but pressure from the Black masses. That pressure will not be satisfied with a few concessions. It demands justice for all sections of the population. Political liberation can be the key to economic emancipation, but only if the political power is in the hands of a party committed to a drastic overhaul of the economic system; otherwise political independence becomes a somewhat fraudulent cover for economic domination.

In economic policy, it is important to realize that there will be many post-liberation restrictions facing black men, as a legacy of a discriminatory society. It would not, for example, be enough simply to remove the restrictions on African land ownership. Africans are too poor to buy land where they like. If all racial barriers on land ownership were removed, Whites, being wealthier, would be able to buy up even African reserved land. Africans must be guaranteed a minimum of land, not because they are black but because they are poor, and poor because of the years of discrimination. The Trekkers took, mostly without payment, the land into which they moved. They defended their ownership by superior force; that land now represents wealth. It is necessary to accept, like Ghana and other African governments, that the

Africa of today needs to apply many of the policies of socialism.

The tiny British territory of Swaziland, which borders on the Eastern Transvaal, gives some idea of the way in which land ownership affects a group's stake in the economy. In Swaziland most of the farms are African; their ownership has been protected. Whenever a White-owned farm is put up for sale, the Swazi nation, through its Paramount Chief and National Council, is able to bid very highly for the property. The Swazi's superior land ownership has laid the foundations of their collective tribal wealth in an economy which, in their case, is still largely agrarian.

Possession of land protected by discriminatory legislation is unfair possession. A job held under protective 'job reservation' laws is a job unfairly held. The Liberal Party has proposed a number of urgent land reforms, aimed at a fairer distribution of land. The government, they demand, must have the power to expropriate, to put a tax on land, and to buy on the open market. These measures must be accompanied by an urgent overhauling of agricultural and pastoral policies. The complete abolition of the pass system, axiomatic to Liberals, would force White farmers to pay salaries competitive with those paid in the cities. The Liberal Party would support legislation for a minimum living wage for Africans, both in the cities and on the land. The Party would not only recognize complete trade union freedom, but help to build up the unions. Liberals are aware of the dangers of raising wages without adding to productivity. But they are also conscious that so long as the state tolerates a cheap labour policy, it will never be enough to ask employers to turn from the use of cheap labour to a more selective use of labour. The state must oblige employers to pay more; and they, in consequence, would be obliged to improve their management policies to survive. Legislation requiring the payment of minimum wages can provide for a phased increase over a period to allow employers to adapt to new conditions. My own view is, however, that much more drastic solutions will be necessary to redress African grievances.

The Liberal Party's acceptance of the need for extra-parliamentary pressure in South Africa evolved gradually. There were two stages. At first there was no more than a detached recognition of a necessity; it was thought that the creation of the pressures was the duty of the oppressed people alone. The Party might possibly provide the vehicle by means of which the change of government would be carried out. Meanwhile, it would remain critically aloof from the squeezing of the Whites, in order to reap the greatest benefit from it. Later, the Party accepted that it must participate directly in 'direct action'.

The role for which it first cast itself falls now to the Progressives. Clearly their expansion will be a temporary setback to the Liberals. The Liberal Party has never been a mass party; its White membership is predominantly middle-class. It has gone through an immense amount of soul-searching to move as far as it has, and this redounds immensely to the credit of its White membership. Few Liberals have deserted to the Progressives, and the membership has accepted the role that the Party has chosen for itself. The Party is multi-racial, and the essence of its belief is that it should provide a working microcosm of the changed South Africa it would like to see.

It was over the question of the use of boycott as a political weapon that the Liberals, as a party, first decided to participate fully in the creation of pressures. The problem first arose when, in 1959, the Party had to consider its attitude towards the A.N.C. proposals to launch a boycott of products of Nationalist firms sold in the Union. Discussions were held with various other groups, mainly from the Congress movement, and the Party eventually agreed that 'in view of the denial of all means of political expression to Africans, Indians and Coloureds, boycott was a legitimate political weapon'. Two months after I arrived in Britain, I was authorized to participate on behalf of the Party in the organization of the A.N.C.-sponsored boycott of South African goods.

If, after white liberals have made all the necessary changes in their attitudes, the gap between them and Africanists remains, it will be because the Africanists are still suffering from the racial slander that libels them as 'inferior'. It will be the duty of the liberals to expose these lies, which should be no difficult task. Their job is to expose them not only to Whites in South Africa and in the rest of the world, but also to the Africans in Africa. It will be necessary to remind people — and not least the Africans — of the achievements of American Negroes, of countless modern Africans, and of the African achievements of the past. It is likely that Afro-Americans, who have been given (by their environment) the greatest opportunities to disprove the slander and have largely done so, will, as they play a greater part in the development of Africa, play an important part in smashing the African inferiority complex; and once it has been smashed by one group of black men, there is a chance that it might be smashed for them all.

I no longer believe — as I once did — that the Liberal Party (or any White liberals) have a really major role to play in the liberation of Africans. They have some role, and certainly a time will come when they will indeed have an important part to play in the country's political life. It will be Africans, however, who will have to take the initiative at this stage and White liberals can only be junior partners. In principle, they must accept African nationalist leadership, remaining neutral for the time being, in the battle between its two sets of exponents. At the present time, the Liberal Party is trying carefully to avoid being banned, and yet it is recruiting African members. This is the old, old story that will make more enemies than friends.

I have discussed, at some length, the policies that liberals might adopt now and the frame of mind which should motivate them, because only if their attitudes are correct will they win African confidence. Their duty is to preach this frame of mind to as many Whites as will listen, inside South Africa, leaving it to Africans to organize the other Africans. Outside, they can persuade the

Whites of the Western world to *act* against South Africa, provided they do so under African leadership and in co-operation with the representatives abroad of both A.N.C. and P.A.C. opinion.

If liberal Whites are to play a conciliatory role in the racial clash of the future — possibly after liberation — they will only be able to do so if their motives were correct before it.

CHAPTER IV

THE BURDEN OF RESPONSIBILITY

O N E certainty stands out from a number of uncertainties about South Africa's future. It is that international action will play an important part in altering the balance of power within the country.

How is power to be transferred from the hands of the White supremacists? We have seen how strongly held are the Afrikaner's innermost convictions and how powerfully White domination is entrenched. A voluntary 'change of heart' can be ruled out completely.

Let us look, then, at the various means by which a revolution could take place from within. Armed revolution? It is important to underline precisely what this means. It would require White military power to be supplanted and immobilized by a superior force, and an unconditional White surrender. If the superior force were not available from within, it would have to be supplemented from abroad.

How would a peaceful revolution come about? The defeat of the present Government is obviously an indispensable requirement. But for whom would they make way and how would they be made to do so? Let us presuppose that by some means or other, internal or external or a combination of both, the country is brought to the verge of complete economic collapse. This also presupposes that there is widespread unemployment among all races, and an imminent danger of the total breakdown of law and order. Will Dr Verwoerd then call in the known African leaders and hand over to them the reins of government? Will the mobs of White unemployed be surrounding the Houses of Parliament and calling for Dr Verwoerd's resignation? Or will they be clashing with Africans, whom they may well blame for the prevailing state of affairs? The question is what Dr Verwoerd would do when he had reached the point at which he could no longer govern. Call an election? Or hand over power to the parliamentary opposition?

It seems probable that, regardless of how drastic the revolution turned out to be, the collapse of White supremacy would come about through a succession of White governments, each shorter and more troubled than the last.

I have already presupposed a great deal. It is now necessary to examine in detail the feasibility either of armed revolution or of the creation of these presupposed conditions. Of course, the revolution would be facilitated if enough Whites could foresee the economic disaster in time, or feel the pinch, or in some way react favourably to the crisis that lay ahead. More and more Afrikaner nationalist voices have been raised against the Government. Some were heard, early on, in the Torch Commando; others when the Senate Act was passed to remove coloured voters from the Common Voters' Roll. There were still more when the Government shirked its responsibilities with regard to territorial segregation and when 'native representation' in parliament was abolished. Among them were leading members of the Dutch Reformed Churches, and in late 1960, dissension in these churches seemed to assume the proportions of a crisis.

'The dogs bark, but the caravan passes on', a Government newspaper once said, using one of Smuts's favourite quotations. In newspapers supporting the United and Progressive Parties these voices of protest are always magnified as portents of a major Afrikaner revolt, with the object of restraining Africans and their White sympathizers — at home and abroad — from drastic action by holding out hope of 'significant' new developments. Those who have protested have been isolated and ostracized by Afrikaner nationalism — 'cast out' from among their people. For example, the crisis of late 1960 was resolved by repudiation by the synods of the Dutch Reformed Churches (with overwhelming majorities) of the stand of the dissentients at the World Council of Churches, and a reaffirmation of belief in apartheid.

The Liberal Party itself once tried to hold out hopes of big changes in White opinion. Optimism, it felt, could be infectious. It thought that by spreading a message of hope it might increase its support, and also the chances of a bloodless internal revolution achieved by constitutional means. It, too, once relied on an Afrikaner intellectual revolt. It said that there was a possibility of a growing conflict of interest within Afrikanerdom. It thought it could show that apartheid placed such a strain on the economy as might eventually destroy it.[1] It had to admit, however, that gold gave South Africa tremendous economic buoyancy. During the Great Depression, gold protected the country from some of the most serious shocks. Today, it gives the Government plenty of leeway for economically disruptive policies. If necessary, the Government could nationalize the gold-mines to counteract the harmful economic effects of apartheid. If the price of gold goes up, this advantage will be correspondingly greater. There can be no doubt that the cumulative ill effects of apartheid on the country's economy could one day produce a great crisis. The crisis of confidence of overseas investors could have an enormous debilitating effect. But I do not believe that these factors alone would be enough to produce the kind of crisis that would succeed in toppling the regime of apartheid.

The Afrikaner revolt might well be of much greater significance once South Africa finds herself in the throes of an economic collapse, but it will have little real effect until other factors have actually created a crisis.

It is abundantly clear that international and internal protest actions have rallied support for the Government, largely because the sanctions and pressures have not yet had their full economic impact and individual material losses have been limited. The threat of loss— without the loss itself — has annoyed people with-

[1] See Appendix

out hurting them. They can still afford to express their indignation by stronger support for the Government.

We are well aware how strongly the Afrikaner believes in his policies. Apartheid is a way of life with religious overtones. The observer may recognize the economic motivation, but the man with the belief and the prejudices cannot himself always examine them so clearly. Many may well — as other ideologists have done — fight to the death for their cause. On the other hand, others may find it necessary to withhold support from the Government because their individual losses are too great. It is an open question which they will do. When that crisis has to be faced, the Afrikaner voices of protest may be meaningful to those who are actually suffering. What is certain is that Afrikaners will dig their heels in until the crisis is upon them. And even then, there is no certainty that in their fanatical belief they will not be ready to drag as many people down with them into the depths of the utmost disaster.

Majority White opinion is hardly likely to facilitate the revolution. But on the other hand, there is a minority White opinion which will behave very differently. Let us dispose quickly of the United Party, the pale shadow of the Nationalists. Its only hope is that the Government will be defeated in a crisis, when it would coalesce with elements of the Nationalist Party to form a new Government, or that enough Nationalist voters, called to vote at a crisis election, would abstain or defect because of heavy personal losses. Such a government might be less drastic than the present one and more amenable to pressure. But it is clear that once the forces of opposition to White supremacy had gathered enough strength to oust Dr Verwoerd, they would continue their pressures on his successors, who would be seeking to apply most of his policies, perhaps a little less harshly.

A smaller minority will turn hopefully towards the Progressive Party, and a handful might look towards the Liberals. Once the crisis had forced the successors to Dr Verwoerd to seek the aid of either of these groups, the end of White supremacy would have begun.

What kind of revolution is it to be?

South Africa has a police force of some twenty thousand Whites and thirty thousand Africans, Indians and Coloureds. The White force is armed with revolvers, sub-machine-guns and Saracen armoured cars. A special constabulary is being established to support the police. There is a sizeable, alert (though not always highly intelligent) special political branch of the police force. This branch can open mail, tap telephones and search houses at any time. It has an intricate system of spies.

There is a permanent army of some twenty thousand men, armed with all modern weapons, including light artillery. It is a highly mobile force, decentralized, with strategic commands spread throughout the country. The air force is well equipped with modern fighters, capable of strafing or bombing townships.

In addition, there is a reserve, the Active Citizen Force (or Territorials), which trains about three thousand men each year, and is organizing 'refresher' courses for reservists. The *ACF* supplements the army, the navy and the air force. On top of these, there are the *skietkomandos* — rifle commandos whose members practise target-shooting regularly. The *skietkomandos* are organized on military lines. As if all this were not enough, 'Mobile Watchers' are being established, to stamp out local disturbances. Paratroopers are being trained to move in on remote trouble spots.

The Union has a small navy and an extensive coastal and border radar system. The whole defence force is designed to put down internal rebellion rather than to repulse external enemies. Heavy and cumbersome equipment has been jettisoned in favour of greater mobility. There will shortly be twelve tank and infantry regiments in strategic parts of the country, equipped with Saracen and Ferret light tanks. South Africa has established her own arms industry, probably in anticipation of an arms embargo. There is a highly developed, modern system of communications.

Against this might, how would armed revolution be organized? Where would it obtain armaments? Where would it set up its bases of operation? The African townships? There are large police-stations in each one. Apartheid has moved most townships some considerable distance from White residential and industrial centres. Strong detachments of police are poised within minutes of them, in well placed police barracks. The special branch detective system has, up to now, known well in advance all contemplated moves.

There are very few rural areas without substantial White populations. Even the native reserves are well covered by government officials. Whenever trouble threatens, many policemen move quickly to the area.

There is little chance of smuggling arms or large numbers of terrorists across the Union's borders. The country is bounded by Angola on the north-west, Rhodesia on the north, and Mozambique on the east. All these are White supremacy countries; gun-runners or terrorists would get short shrift.

Violent revolt in South Africa would be ruthlessly and quickly suppressed. It would result in a great sense of frustration among Africans, and would be a setback to the Opposition. The feeling of depression would last until a new, equally hopeless, spontaneous violent outburst came about, to end only in further frustration.

How successful can an armed underground be, remembering some of the resistance movements in countries occupied by Germany? The answer is another question. What country with twelve million people was occupied by three million Germans, with ninety out of one hundred of the Germans potential agents of their Reich? What of the pattern of the Algerian underground? But what Morocco and Tunisia lie to east and west of the Union?

What about non-violent internal resistance? This includes strikes, civil disobedience, boycott and non-cooperation. Africans could stop depositing money in the Post Office Savings Bank, cut postages and letter-writing to a minimum, keep their children from school, stay away from work, refuse to pay taxes, cut their buying to a minimum, refuse to pay their rents, stop using trains and buses as far as possible, and so on.

There is underground resistance in the Union, but it is very closely watched. Already the major organizations are banned, and there have been prosecutions of members declaring themselves as such — now an offence. There have been isolated outbreaks of violence in the rural areas — near Zeerust, in the Transkei, and elsewhere. The troubles have been ruthlessly and quickly put down.

Non-violence is at its most effective against a Government and a people with a conscience. In the Union, neither has much of that. They do not believe that what they are doing *is* oppression. And if any do, they justify their oppression as a means of survival.

However, the purpose of boycott and strike action — as economic weapons — is to hit directly at White economic privilege; to weaken the economy; if necessary, to ensure that the Whites lose the benefits they get under the system. In principle, if the white man has no specific benefits, he is deprived of the very thing which makes racial domination most worth defending; thereafter his prejudices and religious thinking stand out alone — and they are perhaps more easily assailed when men are not so well off.

African poverty makes boycott a weapon hard to grasp in the Union, because Africans living in poverty must eat and all their spending is absolutely necessary. Strikes require a high level of organization, which we have seen is difficult in the present circumstances. Since official African trade unions are not recognized, such unions as exist have little chance of collecting and saving funds in order to sustain strikers in an illegal strike for any period of time.

Many people outside South Africa are critical of the oppressed peoples of the country for tolerating their oppression for so long; they accuse the subjugated South Africans of not being sufficiently militant, of too much restraint and moderation. Many of these critics have behind them a successful revolt against colonial domination. But not *one* of them has ever faced a task quite so vast as that which faces the dominated human beings of South Africa. It is good to be militant when a cool and deliberate calculation of the odds presents some prospects of success; but it can hardly be good to urge people on to pointless suicide.

The oppressed people will carry on their search to find weapons of internal resistance, but it is clear that international action will be of vital importance in bringing about a change. And not the least importance of each is that it encourages the other.

Those political parties and movements inside South Africa which restrain the search for outside aid and offer themselves as the main hope of change, are doing African liberation a great disservice. The Progressives, for instance, condemn outside aid to Africans in the hope that more Whites will support them in consequence of their actions. They are holding out false hopes and preventing influential people abroad from supporting intervention in the Union.

Is outside intervention in South Africa a wild hope or a real possibility?

South Africa is a running sore in Africa that can poison the feelings towards Whites of people of colour, not only in neighbouring territories, but far beyond its borders. One day, when I was working as a 'griddler' in a Lyons' Corner House in London, I was writing an article for *Contact,* Patrick Duncan's Liberal fortnightly, during the lunch-break. A young West Indian sitting near-by was interested in what I was doing, and I told him what it was. He was very much interested when I told him that I was a South African, and he asked me whether my article was for or against *him.* 'Is it for or against *me?*' were his words. He would probably never even visit South Africa, but because he was not white, what was said and done there concerned *him.* The effects of racial oppression are not confined within the borders of South Africa; they extend far beyond it. No person of colour can stop himself from viewing the South African situation with disgust just because racial domination in the Union is a matter of domestic jurisdiction. A racial insult to an individual is not an insult directed at him alone, but to his group. When these people recall the oppression they have experienced under colonial regimes in

their own countries, and the insults to their colour they must suffer
in the white man's midst in Europe and the United States, who can
blame them for sometimes thinking most white men to be the
same everywhere? South Africa provides a constant reminder to
coloured people all over the world of bitter experiences. African
taunts against European imperialism will have a focal point in
the South African situation for as long as it lasts, and will be an
obstacle in the way of really healthy relationships between Africans
and Whites.

The classic argument for intervention is that the West and the
East are in competition for the friendship of Africa and of the
other uncommitted areas of the world. The West must outbid
Russia if it is to be in a position to win friends and influence Afro-
Asian people.

Already, the Afro-Asians have succeeded in getting acceptance
by the U.N. of a resolution which calls for individual and collective action against South Africa. The question of South-West
Africa is before the International Court of Justice in a manner
which involves the compulsory jurisdiction of the Court. A large
number of countries are applying — or are about to apply —
sanctions against South Africa, and the intensity of feeling against
apartheid inside the Commonwealth virtually forced South Africa
out.

But it is in Western hands that the real power lies to topple Dr
Verwoerd's Government and overthrow White domination. Unfortunately, the countries which have the power to hurt South
Africa are unwilling to use it, while those who wish to do so lack
the economic power, according to Peter Calvocoressi in his book
South Africa and World Opinion. The only exceptions are in the
fields of oil supplies because South Africa gets oil both from
friendly Western countries and hostile Arab states, and in the
labour market since the Union imports a great deal of its labour
on short-term contracts from other African states. The loss of this
labour and an oil embargo could do considerable harm to South

Africa's economy — but not enough. Britain buys more than one-third of South African exports of merchandise, and another substantial slice goes to the White-controlled Federation of Rhodesia, and Nyasaland. The United States, Japan, West Germany, Belgium, Italy and France, in that order, are South Africa's next best customers, though well behind the United Kingdom. Apart from merchandise, South Africa produces vast quantities of gold and a lot of diamonds. (Gold is very difficult to boycott, and so, one would think, are diamonds.) These commodities are exported mainly to Britain and the United States. In addition, British investment in South Africa is estimated to be in excess of one thousand million pounds.

The United Kingdom has been supplying South Africa with arms and armaments, some of which are used by the police to suppress African resistance. The prime duty of the army is to provide a second line of defence to the police, so that the arms they receive are used, not against 'Communist aggression', but mainly against Africans in the Union itself.

It is, of course, possible that a combined Afro-Asian campaign of military intervention in South Africa could take place, but in the Afro-Asians' present state of development, taking account of their commitments elsewhere (in the Congo, for example), it is highly unlikely. The power of the United Nations to enforce effective sanctions depends on Western agreement. Equally, the U.N.'s ability to intervene (say, in pursuance of a resolution to that effect in connection with South-West Africa) must depend on Western agreement.

But it is South Africa's economic interdependence with the West which poses the immediate problem. However much Britain, as the partner in the Western alliance most closely linked to South Africa by economic ties, might feel obliged to expand trade in order to survive, including trade with the Union, there can be little doubt that the maintenance of the economic bonds contributes enormously to the White South Africans' power to maintain their economic and racial domination.

The South African Government has claimed that something like half a million Britons gain a livelihood directly from British exports to South Africa. Almost forty-nine per cent of goods handled at Southampton either come from or go to South Africa. It was this, of course, which underlay the bitter opposition that there was in Britain to the campaign of boycott of South African goods. Various other reasons were given for the opposition, most of them pretexts.

The charge most often made against the boycott was that it would 'most hurt the people it was most meant to help — the Africans'. It was first made by Mr Eric Louw, the South African Minister of External Affairs. His was a new-found concern for the African people. It became the standard pretext for refusal to support the campaign. The Boycott Movement (of which I was the first director) pointed out that the African National Congress had first called for the campaign; that it was (in this matter at least) representative of all politically-conscious African opinion; and that the Africans were better judges of their own interests than Mr Louw. We pointed out that workers who went on strike often had to make some sacrifice, but they did so in the hope that the sacrifice might bring about a redress of their grievances. We added that African resistance in the Union was hamstrung and that an internal boycott was not a weapon available to the Africans, because Africans drew only subsistence wages.

Another argument frequently used was that South Africa's was only one of a number of evil regimes and that it was unfair to single her out. Why not, we were asked, boycott Russian, Spanish or Portuguese goods? Our answer was that there were a number of weapons with which to fight different battles, and the right one had to be chosen for a particular situation. The cold war and the massive deterrent were the weapons against Russia, and increased world trade with her was a means of improving relations with her. Western relations with the Union were good, which was precisely what worried us, because the best weapon against her was to isolate her. As for Portugal and Spain, we knew of no appeal by the oppressed peoples for an international boycott of their country's produce.

It was also argued that the boycott would harm many innocent people in South Africa. The innocent were held to be those among the Whites who voted against the Government. But how much more would they not be harmed by violent racial outbursts, which we were aiming to prevent? Our object was to forge a successful weapon against apartheid that would distract African attention away from violence, give Africans a focus for their hope, and divert them from frustrated bloody outbursts.

One could fairly say that the innocent were on the side of the boycott. Most White opponents of the Government were opposed only because their own rights were being curtailed, and few of them were anything more than mildly critical of some aspects of apartheid. Nor is there much innocence about the many English-speaking leaders in South African politics, industry and commerce who have joined with Nationalists in a 'South African Foundation', whose real purpose is to whitewash apartheid.

On moral grounds, the case against boycott was not very strong. Self-interest operated in this case and the moral argument could make little headway against it. Not only did it provide the real opposition to boycott and sanctions, but it also provided the main motivation for the retention of 'mutually beneficial' bilateral preferential trade links in some new form, now that Commonwealth preferences can no longer apply between the U.K. and South Africa.

It is clear that even if total economic sanctions were applied against South Africa by all the countries of the world, it would still be Britain, with her big sales to South Africa, which would have to bear the brunt of the loss. The position may change if Britain joins the European Common Market and a new pattern of international trade emerges, but as things are, the importance of the South African market to the U.K. will prevent international sanctions from assuming crisis proportions in the South African economy.

Britain has to weigh long-term considerations against short-term ones. To stand out against a growing international insistence on sanctions can lose friends and trade in the future. Even if new trade agreements with South Africa are made, there will be some losses on both sides and some of the old preferences will disappear, marking the start of Britain's disengagement.

It is possible to see a clear pattern of international action against South Africa emerging. The United Nations has already by a majority vote called for 'collective and individual' action against the Union. Very soon, this call must crystallize in a resolution which commits the U.N. itself. Then, of course, the task of working out a practical means of making it effective will devolve on the U.N. Secretariat-General. That task would necessarily include the formulation of trading arrangements which must guarantee the United Kingdom against bearing a disproportionate share of loss. Consideration would also have to be given to the possible temporary drop in additions to the world's gold supplies. In Britain itself, the parliamentary opposition would doubtless press for a rearrangement of trading patterns and for a guarantee fund for investors' losses. The ever-declining confidence in South Africa has almost sealed off all investment already and will lead to the further withdrawal of capital, placing a great strain on the economy.

The effect on South Africa would be an internal political and economic crisis. If the country's economy were weakened, the power of the Whites to oppress would be correspondingly reduced, since armed oppression is an expensive business. Calls are already being made for an arms embargo. If the combination of these factors did not produce the fall of the present regime, then pressure would certainly grow for armed intervention. It would, of course, be so much easier once South Africa's economy was weak, for her power to resist would be that much curtailed.

United Nations' troops are already in South Africa's back garden; as conditions in the Congo improve, they will probably have to move to Angola if the situation there should deteriorate. The next step is into the disputed territory of South-West Africa.

In the meantime, inside South Africa, anti-Whiteism would probably gain strength. Some kind of violence — organized or not — is inevitable, even if those who use it intend only to hasten the moment of intervention.

Of one thing there can be no doubt. If and when the United Nations intervened, it would hardly look kindly on the advancement of an *embittered* African nationalism. That would be contrary to all it stood for. It would seem that the quickest way to secure sanctions would be by the creation of a united non-racial opposition in South Africa; and that boycotts, etc., could be postponed and obstructed if it meant only the unleashing of new destructive racialist forces. The Pan-Africanists of South Africa may refuse to recognize this, but from the moment of a physical intervention, the future would lie in the hands of the U.N. There must eventually come a time for disengagement. And then?

However South Africa changes, it seems distinctly possible that the country will have a period during which Africans will rule the Whites as they have been ruled by them. The Whites might have to put their faith in the same outside world which will have helped the Africans. The fortunes of Black and White people have become entwined in various parts of our earth. Just as there are large White populations in Southern Africa (and elsewhere on the continent), there are large Black populations in the Southern United States and elsewhere in the Americas — as well as in Britain and Europe.

In all three continents, there is a leavening of an Indian and Eurafrican population, and in all three it is the white man who rules. In the Americas and Europe, where Whites are a majority of the population, it is legitimate that they should rule, but not in Africa. The present position will undoubtedly be reversed, preferably as soon as possible.

When that happens, the Blacks of Africa will in a sense have White 'hostages' as an insurance against the maltreatment of

Black people in Europe and America. And the Whites of Europe and America, in their turn, will hold 'hostages' as an insurance against the maltreatment of White people in Africa. It is devoutly to be hoped that the respective majorities will not think of the minorities among them as hostages. I pray that in my own lifetime it may, for instance, be possible for the United States to have a Jew and a Negro as President, not because they are a Jew and a Negro, but because they are the best men for the job, chosen regardless of race.

It is the interdependence of the peoples of the world that I want to stress; it is racialism that I want to eliminate. In a world of human beings — as in any smaller human society — the best guarantee of my own human freedom is the desire of other people that I respect theirs. Their greatest guarantee that I will do so lies in their respect for mine. It is an extension of an old and simple rule: 'Do unto others as you would have them do unto you.' So until there is more charity in the world this principle may have to apply to racial groups. But while the world's races and peoples are as interdependent as they are, one thing is certain: no national boundary will be strong enough to confine the consequences of any racial discrimination.

EPILOGUE

WE have looked closely at the major forces which dominate the South African scene and we have had a glimpse of some of the similarities of the two major nationalist forces. Afrikaner nationalism may well have provided a pattern for African nationalism to follow. Both have had major splits in their history, and the Afrikaner nationalist breakaway movement, more extreme and exclusive than its parent body, moved on to take power which it exercised terribly, each of its leaders giving way to one more extreme.

It is now almost certain that the clash of colour nationalisms will exclude any possibility of a liberal solution. The majority of the Afrikaners (who are also the majority of Whites) firmly believe that they must dominate or be dominated. For most it is a traditional belief; some have recognized that what their people have done has created among Africans the urge to dominate in their turn. But, having realized that, they will do nothing to hasten the inevitable downfall of the Afrikaner. They are tragic figures, those few who feel impelled to go on because what they do is as much the will of God as the consequences of what they do.

Liberals simply do not have the power to get their solution accepted, whether by persuasion, force, or any other course. The majority of Africans have no faith in liberalism and White liberals will have to accept African leadership. An ever-increasing number of White liberals are quitting South Africa in despair — many of them taking their capital out of the country.

The combined forces of opposition do not have the internal strength to overthrow apartheid and White domination immediately. Much less do the liberals. They all seek help from abroad.

Unlike Algeria or the Central African Federation, South Africa has no metropolitan European power to counterbalance and overcome the settler hold over the country. The mood within the country, even if a change is effected by external intervention, is not one amenable to a liberal solution in the immediate future.

We have seen that it is the Western world which now has the physical power to bring about a change. Among many of its people there are now grave doubts and fears about the future course of African nationalism. For these the recent events in the Congo are largely to blame.

But apartheid is so monstrous a policy and so universally condemned that it will not be able to count on the support even of those Whites in the West who are critical of African nationalism. International action of some kind seems inevitable.

Organized violence against apartheid may be attempted inside the country, but many things will militate against it. The strongest factor will be that it will give the Afrikaners a tangible enemy against which they can fight with backs to the wall. The intangible enemy will be economic warfare, and because they cannot fight it from a *laager* of ox-wagons, it will probably succeed in bringing them down. It is said that general elections were held in 1961 mainly because the Government is afraid that by 1963, when elections are normally due, economic crisis might have resulted in disaffection among its supporters.

Black nationalism, like White nationalism, may have to have its hour of glory and its purgation. If the revolution is peaceful and White governments struggle to keep going, succumbing in quicker or slower succession, the prospect of a Black *revanche* will not thereby be diminished. Indeed, the postponement of the prospect might be the very factor ensuring that it comes to fruition, because the spirit of revenge will have more time and reason to spread.

South Africa must have its colour revolution, however long or short its duration may be, and however the change may come about. If it has to be forces of anti-Whiteism which overthrow

White domination, then they will have direct access to power; if the change is peaceful or comes by international action, Africans will still feel a desperate need to assert themselves. Somewhere in the future, there is hope for an end to the agony. Economic realities will shorten the life of any racially exclusive government, and beyond the colour revolution must lie an economic revolution. How long would a Black government last which deliberately excluded from all positions of influence the technical skill that has made South Africa the continent's richest country? Masses of Africans politically awakened in their battle against White domination will not long be satisfied simply with revenge and working out their inferiority complex while the economy stagnates and the promise of economic upliftment remains unfulfilled. South Africa has its technical skill on the spot if only Black and White can learn to live together in non-racialism. If South African Blacks rid themselves of their White oppressors (and their technical skill) they will have to join the long queue for technical aid that exists already, and to which the Congo, Angola, Mozambique and areas of Central Africa will have added. White liberals will have a vital part to play in facilitating racial co-operation when the economic facts make it compulsory, as will the Coloured and Indian people.

Another ray of hope is the spirit of non-racialism that prevails elsewhere in Africa. Of course, there are Black racialists in other African countries, but they are very much a minority. The greatest hope of all is world opinion. If it is a bulwark today against racial domination by Whites, then so will it also be, in time, against any excesses practised by a Black government.

Perhaps I am over-optimistic, but I have a strong faith in world opinion. Of all the possible ways of changing South Africa, I think that international intervention is the strongest. The possibilities of chaos will be enormous in the transition in a country with such deep racial animosities. Only a world force can minimize the bloodshed, control the pillaging, contain the inevitable Afrikaner rearguard guerilla action against the governments of

14

change, and foot the enormous bills that may be necessitated to cope with refugees and losses.

Of course, somehow, some time, South Africa is going to have to work out her own destiny. She has already produced many great men. Perhaps her greatest are still to come.

APPENDIX

APPENDIX

On July 14th *and* 20th, 1959, *the* Rand Daily Mail *published two articles in which I had discussed the effects of apartheid on the economy.*

Fewer Jobs — Lower Output — Less Money
POLICIES THAT CAUSE WASTE AND LOSS

The Union is, at present, busy nosing its way out of slump conditions. Their effects were not greatly harmful but a warning has been sounded for us all.

There are all sorts of established factors governing the state of any economy, including the effects of conditions in other countries. But in the Union race policies have their own special effect. The Government has made it quite clear that it will not be deterred by economic factors from applying apartheid.

What are the effects of this attitude on the economy?

There is, for instance, the policy of establishing industries on the borders of the reserves. The result has been the use of cheap labour and the undercutting of prices of goods made in the urban areas. Because employers in urban areas cannot compete, factories have had to close down. Urban workers lose their jobs, and rural workers are miserably paid. This means that there is a great deal less money in circulation.

Then there is the policy of job reservation, which is designed to 'protect' White workers from competition by reserving certain classes of work for people of a specified race. This means that the expansion of an industry must depend on the increase in the number of White workers available. People of other races cannot even be trained for the jobs that are reserved in this way.

213

The policy is based on the fact that an African would be paid less than a White man even for the same work, and that, in open competition the White man would either have to accept less money or lose the job. Instead of creating conditions which would enable the African's standards to be raised, a barrier to his progress is laid down.

This means that a limit is placed on the earning power of masses of Africans whose skills might mean greater productivity if properly used, and better wages. That would increase demand. It also means that there are minimum salaries for all Whites, no matter how unproductive they may be. Protected from competition, the White workers do not have that incentive to produce more which the competitive element always provides.

The Group Areas Act is another costly piece of legislation disrupting the economy. A large number of Indian retailers have come under the axe. Wholesalers and manufacturers immediately restrict credit, and accordingly they buy less and stock less.

The cost of apartheid on buses can be enormous. It means in simple terms that two buses must run on the same route even if neither is filled. Cape Town's bus company must be subsidized to apply this policy, though previously it could make a profit. Pietermaritzburg is unable to afford the cost of bus apartheid. The state must pay the subsidy, and so taxes rise again.

The whole economy is geared to racial separation and therefore to the duplication of services. This often means two officials where one would otherwise have been adequate. It must not be thought that because there are more officials there is more money in circulation. Their productivity is the test. They themselves are not engaged in activity that is producing more money.

The Government's ideological legislation has brought great increases in unproductive work. Scores of little things all add up to millions of pounds. There is the Population Register, the Senate, the administration of the pass system and the imprisonment of hundreds of thousands of petty offenders, the great increase in the number of policemen involved in this work, and the increased work of the courts. In this category can be included the number of man hours lost by those who are imprisoned for petty offences.

Our economy has so far been sufficiently resilient to absorb the effect of these policies. The recent downward trend has shown clearly, however, that when economic factors begin to bring about a slump, the strains imposed on the economy by the political factors aggravate the situation enormously. A situation could well arise where the cumulative effects of race policies over a period would become greater than the economy can stand, in which case the political factors could become the direct cause of a recession.

* * *

Higher Wages and Higher Output
THE PARALLEL ROADS OF PROGRESS

If African wage and living standards remain depressed, then the nation is closing to itself avenues for the immense expansion of its economy.

First, a ceiling is placed on the development of what now is an immense potential market for industrial products.

But poverty wages also have negative effects most harmful to the economy. They produce undernourishment and create conditions for disease. And they limit the productivity of the workers.

Today the African is increasingly integrated in our economy. It is Government policy to try to 'disintegrate' him and to treat him as a separate factor. This is extremely dangerous. African development is an important element of national progress. It will ensure increasing prosperity in the whole economy, with widening scope for gainful employment of workers of all races.

But one thing must be made clear. All economists agree that any general increase in wages without an increase in productivity produces no addition to living standards and no gain whatsoever. Although people may get more money, they can buy no more with that money.

Mr H. R. Fraser of the Association for the Improvement of Wages and Productivity of Bantu Workers has stated this clearly: 'Add x million pounds to wages and you add x million pounds to costs, so that with x million pounds increase in prices, the increased wages will still only buy the same volume of goods.'

The S. A. Institute of Race Relations has made exhaustive surveys of African expenditure on essential items. For a family of five, the monthly cost of six essentials — food, rent, fuel and light, transport, clothing and tax, amounted to £23. 10s. 4d. in 1954. It was just over £27 in 1958. These are absolute essentials.

The Institute has shown that in 1954, the average income of such a family was £15. 18s. 11d. Since 1954 the average wage increase per month has been nowhere higher than £1. 10s. The monthly deficit for the average family of a man, his wife and three children was a little more than £9 in 1958. This simply means cutting down on food.

The chairman of a Wage Determination Board states his problem, as does Mr Fraser's Association, to be how to raise wages 'without endangering the economy of the country'.

Neither has perhaps taken sufficiently into account the negative effects of poverty wages. There is a certain scope for the immediate increase of wages that is determined by this negative factor. If the burden and the worry of undernourishment were removed at once, Africans would immediately produce more. A fairly substantial increase could take place at the moment, not only without endangering the economy, but on the contrary, with widespread beneficial results.

There are several stages towards placing African wages above the 'poverty datum line'. The first increase must eliminate the negative effects of poverty and so enable Africans to produce the maximum even in existing conditions.

The second stage must be co-ordinated with management's use of methods to increase productivity and to eliminate unproductivity where it is found. Even if some people lose their jobs, provided that wages and productivity are increasing, the economy will be stimulated and with expanding production, those people would be absorbed elsewhere. These improvements must fit into a general plan, for which, if the Government will not assume responsibility, organized commerce and industry must.

Mr Fraser has said this of management techniques: 'Methods must be improved, jobs must be evaluated, aptitudes must be tested and each man used to best advantage, incentives must be offered, men must be trained for new types of work — the operation of mechanized equipment, for example.'

These are steps which can be taken independently of Government policy. But there must also be continual public pressure on the Government to change its policies, and education of the public about their dangers to the economy.

Africans must be allowed to develop skills, but job reservation prevents this and a ceiling is placed on the expansion of the economy. African trade unions cannot be registered; this puts them at the mercy of employers. Besides this, they are voteless. Trade union bargaining has raised wages in other countries without disrupting national economies; rather it has stimulated them in the long run.

Mr Alex Hepple says in his pamphlet *Poverty Wages* that overseas markets may one day say of our goods that they are produced by sweated labour and so have an excellent reason for imposing higher import duties on the grounds of unfair competition.

Promises were made two years ago at the time of the bus boycott which have not really been kept. Does the White man always appear to break his promises?

INDEX

INDEX

INDEX

political parties, *see* Labour Party, Liberal Party, National Party, Progressive Party, United Party
Pondoland, 144
'poor Whites', 91, 92, 93, 112, 115, 125-6
'positive action', 154-5, 161, 164
poverty, of Africans, 113-15, 117, 144, 187-8
Predestination, influence of concept on Afrikaner thought, 62, 68, 101, 207
press, freedom of the, 136-8
Progressive Party, 153, 185, 189, 195, 196
Protectorates, 139

RACE RELATIONS, S. AFRICAN INSTITUTE OF, 114
republicanism, 81, 87, 105
reserves, *see* Native reserves
Retief, Piet, 68, 69, 72
Rhodes, Cecil John, 74
Rhodesias, 73

SANCTIONS, 200-1, 203, 205
Sekhukuneland, 144
Senate, *see* Parliament
Sharpeville, 47, 124, 132, 133, 135, 136, 165, 167, 168, 179
Shooting at Sharpeville, 166
slaves and slavery, 60, 67, 71, 72, 73; abolition of, 68, 71, 72
Smuts, Gen. J. C., 75, 76, 78, 79, 80, 87, 88, 89, 92, 100, 108
Sobukwe, R. M., 172, 176, 179
socialism, 152, 162, 167, 188
social welfare, 123
Somerset, Lord Charles, 64, 71
Sophiatown, 39, 123-4
South African
    Broadcasting Corporation, 138
    Bureau of Racial Affairs, 99, 100
    Institute of Race Relations, 114
    Party, (*see also* United Party), 76, 79
    Police, *see* police
    United Front, 54, 168
South-West Africa, 78, 106, 108
Strijdom, J. G., 98, 101, 119
strikes, 113, 115, 132, 155, 169, 198
sugar farming, 14, 84
Swart, C. R., 89, 135, 136
Swaziland, 48, 49, 50, 51, 139, 188

TOMLINSON COMMISSION, 139-40, 143-4
Torch Commando, 108-9
trade unions, 113, 129, 188, 198
Transkei, 144-5, 198
Transvaal, 65, 73, 77, 79, 85, 90, 108; Republic, 73, 74
Treason Trial, 39, 132, 167
Treaties ceding land, 65, 66, 69
Trekker (*see also* Boer, Voortrekker), 60, 68, 72, 73, 91, 104, 111, 120; influence of religion on, 61-3, 68, 97; clashes over land between Africans and, 64-7, 69

UITLANDERS, 74, 81, 106
Union, Act of, *see* Acts of Parliament (South Africa)
Union, Settlement of, 75, 79, 85
Unionists, 76, 77, 79, 80, 81, 85, 149
United Front, S. African, 54, 168
United Nations, 26, 27, 169, 183, 200, 201, 204, 205
United Party, 89, 93, 106, 108, 127, 153, 195
United States, *see* America
universities, 105, 118, 119, 120

VERWOERD, DR H. F., 24, 98, 101, 116, 117, 118, 136, 139, 141, 142, 143, 195
Voortrekker (*see also* Boer, Trekker), 20, 70, 95, 116
Voortrekker Monument, 19, 102
voters' roll, 88, 106, 107-11, 160, 193

WAGES, of Africans, 113, 114, 115
Western world, in relation to Africa and S. Africa, 182, 183, 190, 201, 208
White: domination, 67, 68, 70, 72, 93, 97, 100, 158, 160, 185, 192, 195, 201, 209; privilege, 97, 98, 111, 112, 113, 161, 175
Witwatersrand, 74, 85, 114
World Wars, 77, 78, 80, 81, 88, 89, 161

XHOSA, 64, 66, 67, 82, 83, 111, 118, 119, 120

ZEERUST, 144, 198
Zulu, 64, 68, 69, 70, 84, 95, 120

This book may be kept

~~FOURTEEN DAYS~~

A fine will be charged for each
day the book is kept overtime.

FEB 16 '68			
MAY 1 '68	MAY -2 1988		
NOV 27 '69			
DEC 9 '69			
MAY 23 '70			
DEC 8 '70			
NOV 29 '72			
FEB 27 '73			
APR 25 '73			
MAY 15 '74			
MAY 30 '74			
MAY 26 '78			
APR 23 '78			
APR 13 '78			
MAY 23 1978			

Demco 291–F5